Little Red Book
of
Effective Speaking Skills

Other Titles in the Series

Little Red Book of SMS Slang and Chat Room Slang	Little Red Book of Synonyms
	Little Red Book of Antonyms
Little Red Book of English Vocabulary Today	Little Red Book of Common Errors
	Little Red Book of Letter Writing
Little Red Book of Grammar Made Easy	Little Red Book of Essay Writing
	Little Red Book of Word Fact
Little Red Book of English Proverbs	Little Red Book of Spelling
	Little Red Book of Language Checklist
Little Red Book of Prepositions	Little Red Book of Perfect Written English
Little Red Book of Idioms and Phrases	
Little Red Book of Phrasal Verbs	Little Red Book of Punctuation
Little Red Book of Euphemisms	Little Red Book of Reading and Listening Skills
Little Red Book of Word Power	
Little Red Book of Modern Writing Skills	Little Red Book of A Child's First Dictionary
	Little Red Book of Phonics

Little Red Book *of* Effective Speaking Skills

Terry O'Brien

Published by
Rupa Publications India Pvt. Ltd 2011
7/16, Ansari Road, Daryaganj
New Delhi 110002

Sales centres:
Bengaluru Chennai
Hyderabad Jaipur Kathmandu
Kolkata Mumbai Prayagraj

Copyright © Terry O'Brien 2011

All rights reserved.
No part of this publication may be reproduced, transmitted,
or stored in a retrieval system, in any form or by any means,
electronic, mechanical, photocopying, recording or otherwise,
without the prior permission of the publisher.

P-ISBN: 978-81-291-1852-3
E-ISBN: 978-81-291-2501-9

Sixteenth impression 2025

20 19 18 17 16

The moral right of the author has been asserted.

Typeset by Innovative Processors, New Delhi.

Printed in India

This book is sold subject to the condition that it shall not, by way of
trade or otherwise, be lent, resold, hired out, or otherwise circulated,
without the publisher's prior consent, in any form of binding or cover
other than that in which it is published.

*I dedicate this book to late Prof. A.P. O'Brien,
my father, friend, guide and mentor, who
inspired me to the canon of excellence:
re-imagining what's essential*

PREFACE

Improving your English speaking skills will help you communicate more easily and effectively. But how do you become a more confident English speaker?

Practise where you can, when you can.

It's important to build your confidence. If possible, use simple English sentence structure that you know is correct, so that you can concentrate on getting your message across.

Try to experiment with the English you know. Use words and phrases you know in new situations.

Try to respond to what people say to you. You can often get clues to what people think by looking at their body language. Respond to them in a natural way.

Try NOT to translate into and from your own language. This takes too much time and will make you more hesitant.

If you forget a word say things that 'fill' the conversation. This is better than keeping completely silent. Try using **um**, or **er**, if you forget the word.

Don't speak too fast! It's important to use a natural rhythm when speaking English, but if you speak too fast it will be difficult for people to understand you.

Try to relax when you speak – you'll find your mouth does most of the pronunciation work for you. When you speak

English at normal speed, you'll discover that many of the pronunciation skills, such as linking between words, will happen automatically.

Remember, when speaking English…

Try to become less hesitant and more confident.

Don't be shy to speak – the more you do it, the more confident you'll become.

Remember to be polite – use **"please"** and **"thank you"** if you ask someone to do something for you. So here we begin with the 3S factor of speaking:

Stand up
Speak up
Shut up

Best of luck!

Terry O'Brien

PART I

Stand Up

Fear is actually the adrenalin in a person to be an effective speaker. It is the desire to communicate effectively. Winston Churchill, a landmark speaker of his times, was once asked by a journalist why he sweated a lot on reaching the podium for addressing the public. Was it fear? He rightly retorted: "This is the sweat of perfection!"

How to Conquer Public Speaking Fear

Public speaking is a common source of stress for everyone. Public speaking, however, IT DOES NOT HAVE TO BE STRESSFUL!

You have to overcome the fear of public speaking. You have to keep **ten key principles** always in mind.

There are **eleven "hidden" causes of public speaking stress**.

Key Principles

Principle 1—Speaking in Public is NOT Stressful

Public speaking is NOT stressful. Thousands of human beings have learned to speak in front of groups with little or no stress at all. Many of these people were initially terrified to speak in public. Their knees would shake, their voices would tremble, their thoughts would become jumbled. Yet they learned to eliminate their fear of public speaking completely.

If they can conquer the fear of public speaking, so can you! It just takes the right guiding principles, the right understanding, and the right plan of action to make this goal a reality.

It's not difficult.

Principle 2—You Don't Have to be Brilliant or Perfect to Succeed

You don't have to be brilliant, witty, or perfect to succeed. That is not what public speaking is all about. You can be average. You can be below average. You can make mistakes, get tongue-tied, or forget whole segments of your talk. You can even tell no jokes at all and still be successful.

It all depends on how you, and your audience, define "success." Your audience doesn't expect perfection.

The essence of public speaking is this: *give your audience something of value*. That's all there is to it. If people in your audience walk away with something or anything of value, they will consider you a success. If they walk away feeling better about themselves, feeling better about some job they have to do, they will consider you a success. If they walk away feeling happy or entertained, they will consider their time with you worthwhile.

Even if you pass out, get tongue-tied, or say something stupid during your talk . . . they won't care! As long as they get something of value, they will be thankful.

They don't even need to feel good to consider you a success. If you criticize people, or if you stir them up to ultimately benefit them, they might still appreciate you, even though you didn't make them feel good at the time.

Principle 3—All You Need is Two or Three Main Points

You don't have to deliver heaps of facts or details to give your audience what they truly want. While you may choose to include lots of facts and information, you only need to make two or three main points to have your talk be successful. You can even have your whole talk be about only one key point.

Principle 4—You also Need a Purpose That is Right for the Task

This principle is very important. One big mistake people make when they speak in public is they have the wrong purpose in mind. Often, they have no specific purpose in mind; this unconsciously causes a whole lot of unnecessary stress and anxiety.

This what is termed a "hidden cause" of public speaking stress.

You may be good but someone is going to disapprove of either you or your argument. That is just human nature. In a large group of people, there will always be a diverse opinions, judgments, and reactions. Some will be positive, others will be negative.

If you do a lousy job, some people will sympathize with you and feel for you, while others will criticize you ruthlessly. If you do a fantastic job, someone will resent your ability and might disapprove of you on that basis alone. Some people will leave early because of an emergency. Some will fall asleep because they are tired. So never attempt to get everyone in your audience to think well of you.

The essence of public speaking is to give your audience something of value. The essence here is GIVE not GET! The purpose of public speaking is not for you to *get* something (approval, fame, respect, sales, clients, etc.) from your audience. It is to *give* something useful to your audience.

If you focus on giving as much as you can to your audience, you will then be aligned with the truth about public speaking. You also will avoid one of the biggest pitfalls that cause people to experience public speaking anxiety.

Principle 5—The Best Way to Succeed is Not to Consider Yourself a Public Speaker!

The best way to succeed as a public speaker is not to consider oneself as a public speaker at all.

We often assume that to be successful ourselves, we must strive very hard to bring forth certain idealistic qualities we presently lack.

The problem is that we try to become someone other than ourselves! We try to be a public speaker, whatever that image means to us.

The truth about public speaking is that most successful speakers got that way by being themselves They didn't try to be like somebody else. Sincerity and authentic is the bottom line of public speaking, in fact at any level of communication. They just were themselves in front of other people. It is then that they discovered how much fun they could have doing something most other people dread.

Don't try to become public speakers! No matter what type of person we are, or what skills and talents we possess, we can stand up in front of others and fully be ourselves.

In public speaking we can fully be ourselves in the presence of others. One can be bold, compassionate, silly, informative, helpful, witty, anything one wants. One can tell jokes, tell humorous or poignant anecdotes, or do anything else that feels natural in the moment.

The speaker is alive; the speaker is geared up. He is fully invested in everything he says and does. That's another gift a speaker can give to his audience. It also allows him to tell when he has gone on too long or when the people who are listening to him begin to stray away.

Sometimes, we enjoy throwing ourselves in front of a group without knowing specifically what one's going to say. The speaker could just focus on his three main points and remember he is there to give people something of value. In many instances, he will say things he'd never said before! They just come out of him spontaneously while "being with his audience."

Don't try to give talks the way one does, or the way anyone else does. Just go out there, armed with a little knowledge and a few key points, and be yourself. Everything else will usually work out.

Principle 6—Humility and Humour

Humility and humour, can go a long way to making your talks more enjoyable and entertaining for your audience.

If being humorous feels comfortable for you, or if it fits your speaking situation, go for it. It usually works, even if you don't do it perfectly.

Humility means standing up in front of others and sharing some of your own human frailties, weaknesses, and mistakes. We all have weaknesses, and when you stand up in front of others and show that you're not afraid to admit yours, you create a safe, intimate climate where others can acknowledge their personal shortcomings as well. But beware: Don't begin your talk with the cliche: "I couldn't prepare this talk as I was busy but I will talk on . . . " This will be a confession that you are here to waste time.

Being humble in front of others makes you more credible, more believable, and paradoxically more respected. People can connect with you more easily. You become "one of them". It also sets a tone of honesty and self-acceptance. True humility is easily distinguished from the pretense of acting humble. If you pretend, your audience will perceive this and lose respect for you.

Humour and humility can be combined very effectively. Telling humorous stories about yourself, or using your own personal failings to demonstrate some point you are trying to make, can be both entertaining and illuminating.

If you get nervous when you stand up to speak in front of a group, don't hide this fact from your audience. Be real—and humble—by acknowledging your fear openly and honestly.

You can start your talk with a humorous story that produces the same effect. Try wit also: "tough reasonableness". This is an intellectual quality. Humour has an undercurrent of feeling.

Principle 7—Believe: When You Speak in Public, Nothing "Bad" Can Ever Happen!

One thing that adds to the fear of public speaking is the fear people have that something awful, terrible may happen.

There is fear: what if they all get up and leave after the first ten minutes? What if theu put harsh questions or comments once I'm done? What if someone in the audience tries to turn the group against me?

Most of them don't happen. Even when they do, it's useful to have a strategy in mind.

Most of the "negative" things that happen when one is speaking can be handled by keeping one principle in mind: everything that happens can be used to one's advantage.

"If people get up and start to head for the door, I can stop what I'm doing and ask for feedback." Was there something about my topic, my style, or my manner of presentation that was offensive to them? "Were they simply in the wrong room at the start and didn't know it?" Did someone misinform them about what my talk was going to cover?

Even if everyone walked out and refused to give a reason, one could ultimately find ways to benefit from this experience.

Principle 8—You Don't Have to Control the Behavior of Your Audience

To succeed as a public speaker, you don't have to control the behavior of your audience. You do need to control—your own thoughts, your preparation, arrangement for audio-visual aids, how the room is laid out—but one thing you don't have to control is your audience.

If people are restless, don't try to control this. If someone is talking to a the person next to him, or reading the newspaper, or falling asleep, leave them alone. If people look like they aren't paying attention, refrain from criticizing them.

Principle 9—In General, the More You Prepare, the Worse You Will Do

Preparation is useful for any public appearance.

If you have the wrong focus (i.e., purpose), if you try to do too much, if you want everyone to applaud your every word, if you fear something bad might happen or you might make a minor mistake, then you can create stress for yourself. In this case the more effort you put in, the worse you probably will do.

Remember if you know your subject well, or if you've spoken about it many times before, you may only need a few minutes to prepare sufficiently. All you might need is to remind yourself of the two or three key points you want to make.

Over preparation usually means you don't feel confident about your ability to speak about it in public. You'll need to develop trust in your natural ability to speak successfully. Solicit opportunities to speak on your subject in public. If you have something of value to tell others, keep getting in front of people and deliver it. In no time at all, you'll gain confidence.

Principle 10—Your Audience Truly Wants You to Succeed

The last principle to remember is that your audience truly wants you to succeed. Most of them are scared of public speaking, just like you. They know the risk of embarrassment, humiliation, and failure you take every time you present yourself in public. They feel for you. They will admire your courage. The audience will be on your side, no matter what happens.

Review of 11 Hidden Causes of Public Speaking Stress

1. Thinking that public speaking is stressful (it's not).
2. Thinking you need to be brilliant or perfect to succeed (you don't).
3. Trying to impart too much information or cover too many points in a short presentation.
4. Having the wrong purpose in mind.
5. Trying to please everyone (this is unrealistic).
6. Trying to emulate other speakers (very difficult) rather than simply being your true self (very easy).
7. Failing to be personally revealing and humble.
8. Being fearful of potential negative outcomes.
9. Trying to control the wrong things such as the behavior of your audience.
10. Spending too much time over preparing (instead of developing confidence and trust in your natural ability to succeed).
11. Thinking your audience will be as critical of your performance as you might be.

Review of 10 Key Principles to Always Keep in Mind

1. Speaking in Public is NOT Stressful
2. You Don't Have to be Brilliant or Perfect to Succeed
3. All You Need is Two or Three Main Points
4. You also Need a Purpose that is Right for the Task
5. The Best Way to Succeed is NOT to Consider Yourself a Public Speaker!

6. Humility and Humor Can Go a Long Way
7. When You Speak in Public, Nothing "Bad" Can Ever Happen!
8. You Don't Have to Control the Behavior of Your Audience
9. In General, the More You Prepare, the Worse You Will Do
10. Your Audience Truly Wants You to Succeed

Dos and Don'ts in Public Speaking

Dos	Don'ts
<ul><li>Prepare your speed</li><li>Practice</li><li>Relax</li><li>Start your speech with a punch line</li><li>Say it like you mean it</li></ul>	<ul><li>Don't read out your speech or learn your speech by heart</li><li>Don't apologise</li><li>Don't use slides with too much info</li><li>Don't fall in love with the sound of your voice</li><li>Don't lean while speaking; maintain eye contact</li></ul>

PART II

Speak Up

"I keep 6 honest serving men (they taught me all I knew). Their names are **WHAT – WHY – WHEN – HOW – WHERE – WHO**."

WHAT & WHY: Deciding the Objective

General Objective	*Specific Objective*
Fall into one category To persuade or sell To teach To stimulate thought To inform To entertain*	The *Specific Objective* will depend on the **Subject Matter** entirely.

*Whatever be your *General Objective* there is our always need to try and **ENTERTAIN** your audience.

This does not mean cracking jokes. It means that the material must be put over in such a way that it is interesting and people want to listen.

Note: It is an excellent idea to write down the objective of the speech in one sentence. This has various benefits:
- It clears the speaker's mind right at the start.
- When your notes are complete you can again check that you are meeting your original aim.

WHO: Researching the Audience

Audience – most important people in the whole exercise. What should you know about them?

- How many of them are there?
- Why are they there – Are they there of their own free will? Were they sent to listen? Are they paying?
- What is their present knowledge of the subject of the talk.
- Are they likely to have any bias towards or against the subject or speaker.
- What are their expectations of the talk and the speaker.
- What age range and sex are they.

The bottom line: **Response-ability**

Pitch Your Speech at the Right Level

A woman talking to a group of men about women's equality will be different when talking to a group of women. Similarly a computer expert talking to experts and novices will be different.

WHERE: Preparing the Environment

Important to consider where the talk is going to take place.
The following points need consideration.
Practising – Size of room aligned with volume of voice.

HOW: How things in the room work

- Distractions – become aware of any likely distractions for you and your audience.
- Possibility of noise/general interruption.

WHEN: Timing

- Time of the day – after lunch is known as the 'Graveyard' session in training circles.
- How long have we got – keeping to time.
- Right amount of material for the talk. If there is no clock in the room, take our watch off and put it on a table.

SEATING
(May vary)

Theatre Style	Horseshoe	Curved	Cabaret Rows
Sit in rows	(horseshoe shape)	(curved lines)	(groups around tables)
Formal atmosphere and eye contact with the audience more difficult to achieve.	Single row of people arranged in a horseshoe shape. Informal and conducive to participation.	Similar problems as with the theatre style but slightly less formal.	People sitting in groups around tables. Useful if you break the audience into formal discussion groups.

Points to Watch

- Back-benchers – most people have a tendency of having too many chairs – rope off the back rows.

- Ideally you want the audience as near as possible.
- Try to make sure the seats are not too comfortable. Low, soft chairs can be sleep inducing – the last thing you want from the audience.
- The environment you have to speak in can either hinder or help. The aim is to minimize the hindrances and maximize the good points.

Concentration Problems

Concentration hard for long is often difficult.
Concentration level – 2 hour period.

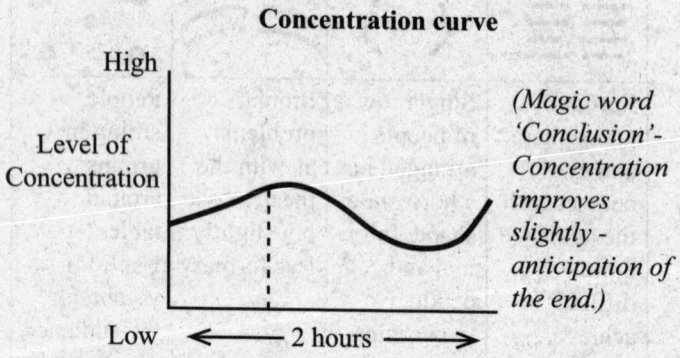

Concentration Curve

Concentration is good for the first 20 minutes or so. It becomes harder after that.

Checklist -1

General Preparation

- Why am I speaking? Clarify objective
- Who am I speaking to? Research the audience.
- Where am I speaking? Familiarize yourself with the venue and equipment. Practice your voice. Anticipate distractions. Arrange the seating suitably.
- When am I speaking? Time of the day? How long have I got? Anticipate lack of concentration.

Preparing the Material

- Any speech will almost certainly fail unless careful thought is given to the subject matter.

The following stages of activities will help your thought process in the preparation of the material and ensure that your speech is well structured and lively.

Stage One: Brainstorming

- Essential to get all thought and ideas on your subject down on paper; useful method – make pattern notes.
- Take a plain sheet of paper. Write the objectives of your talk at the top and the main terms of your talk in the centre of the page in a circle.
- Write down all the ideas and thoughts you have on the subject, starting from the circle and branching out along lines of connecting ideas.
- Let your mind be as free as possible. Do not restrict your thought by deciding where each point should go in a list. Your ideas should flow easily.

16 Little Red Book of Effective Speaking Skills

- When finished, circle any related ideas and sections and establish your order of priorities and organization.

COMPLETED PATTERN NOTE

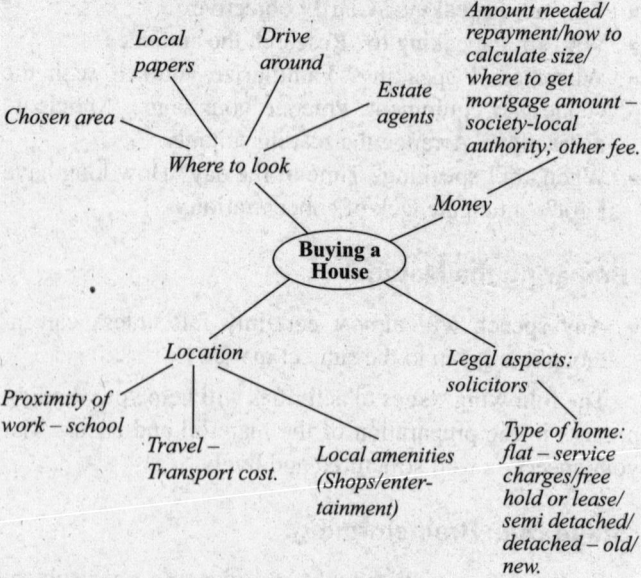

Stage Two: Structuring and Selecting

- Important to keep the number of main points to a minimum.
- In a 45 minutes speech you should not try to make more than 7 main points :
- In a 5 minute speech – 1 or 2 main points.
- You should concentrate on and write the middle of the speech first.
- Objective

- Audience
- How long have I got?
- MUST, SHOULD, COULD – Basis- what the audience is.
- <u>Must tell</u> – How it will operate.
- <u>Should</u> – Why the decision to install.
- <u>Could</u> – Why this system has been chosen against any other.

Stage Three: Illustrating

- As a speaker – talk in picture; create mental images.

Stage Four: Opening and Closing

Introduction: The introduction can be looked like this :

I	⟶	Interest
N	⟶	Need
T.	⟶	Title
R	⟶	Ratings
O	⟶	Objectives

Interest: Find something to capture the attention of the audience immediately. Preferably not the usual lines like : 'unaccustomed as I am to public speaking ———— .

Need: Show the audience why they <u>need</u> to listen. Its relevance.

Title and Rating: Tell them the subject of your talk and what you are going to cover.

Objective: Objective should shine through to your audience.

CLOSING:

- Should be conclusive. It should not just drift to a halt with words like 'I think that's all I've got to say'.
- Remember that what you say in the end is the last thought you leave with your audience.
- Summarise you main points again.

Note: It is essential to write out your opening and closing sentences in full and incorporate them into your notes. The opening sentence will help to get you started and when you have uttered the closing lines you will know you have come to the end, hence avoid to drift to a halt.

Stage Five: Notes

- Notes should be brief and consist of keywords.
- Speakers who use verbatim notes are really reading out aloud rather than speaking from within. Also completely written out speeches sound stilted even if learned by heart. This is because written English and Spoken English are not the same.
- If you are making a particular important speech, it is an excellent idea to write the whole thing out in full, practice and then reduce it all to key notes – so that you are able to look at the audience.
- Notes are best – put on cards. There are various good reasons for this:
  - They do not shake around as much as sheets of paper if you are nervous.
  - You do not need a lectern to prop up all the sheaves of paper, as cards can be held quite easily.
  - Since they are smaller, they encourage you to use key words rather than writing down complete sentences.

Checklist – 2

Preparing the Material

- Brainstorm the subject: Make pattern notes.
- Structure and Select – keep the number of main points down to an appropriate level.
- Select on the basis of – objective, time, audience, must, should, could.
- Tell it like the news – tell them what you are going to tell – tell them what you've told them.

Use illustrations

- Simplify difficult or complex information. Use real life examples to illustrate points.

Opening and closing

- Write opening and closing sentence in full.
- Be challenging and capture the audience in the opening.
- Be conclusive when you finished.
- Notes – Notes on cards; use key words; writing timings and messages to yourself own cards; clip them together.

Putting Yourself Across

3 Vs

Verbal – *to do with words.*
Vocal – *to do with tone of voice.*
Visual – *to do with facial expression, gesture, posture and so on.*

Graded Priority of 3Vs

7% Verbal – to do with words.
38% Vocal – to do with tone of voice.
55% Visual – to do with facial expression, gesture, posture and so on.

Words

- Use concrete, simple language. Do not talk in abstractions. Do not use 5 words when one would do: e.g. "in the fullness of time" i.e. "soon" or "now".
- Be conscious of using positive words. Avoid words like "but", "try", "may be" etc.
- Talk in sentences and beware of different level of abstractions – Gauri, the cow:

Wealth
Farm assets
Cow
Gauri

(Keep towards the lower level of the ladder.)

How We Say It

- Expression – Emphasis placed on particular words.
- Pausing – do not be afraid of pausing.
- Tone of voice and pitch – tedious – a speech delivered in a monotonous tone of voice.
- A voice that moves up and down like a piano scale.
- Speak clearly – Be careful of tongue twisting words.

Speak Out, Not Up

Be loud enough for the room. Breathing properly can help here. Lungs are like an organ. If you do not put enough air into them you get a rather squeaky sound out.

Body language/look at the audience/smile – audience smiles back/avoid creating barriers/stand square – feet slightly apart – avoid leaning and keep hands out of pockets.

Problems to be watched while Brainstorming

- May end up with too much information.
- You may set yourself with lot of editing work.
- Risk not to focus on your presentation.
- May end up with unrelated points.

Tips for Correct Speaking

When you speak, remember there are **two aspects**:
 (i) *What you say*
 (ii) *How you say*

Good Morning: Can be said
- Lovingly
- perfunctorily
- grumpily
- angrily

'*A good morning*' can relieve morning weariness, can brighten the entire office staff, can raise eyebrows or lower them. It is amazing what speaking just two words can do or undo.

"*I need your help*" says your boss walking up to your desk. Is it an *order*, is it a *command* or a *request*, a *routine order* or is it a *welcome compliment*.

Conversation, in part, is **self-expression**. It provides us opportunities for asserting our individuality, telling the world just how we feel, or "letting off steam".

At its best **conversation** means the **pooling of information, the sharing of interests, the bringing together of ideas.**

Each one of us has a life of personal appearances – there will be a time when all eyes are on us, the pin-pointed individual who has to speak alone across a crowded room. You not only have to hold your job down to your own satisfaction, but appear to be doing it well before those in your charge. If you are hesitant or limited in vocabulary, you may well not do justice to the most brilliant schemes you present. **SPEECH IS A FORM OF SELF PORTRAIT**.

Speech making falls into two categories:

Personal	Technical
Construct entirely from your own material, adapted to meet the requirements of a general brief on a social occasion.	The ingredients, the *data, surveys, figures* are prepared – do your best to **HUMANISE** them.

For this we need:
- *GOOD WORKING **VOCABULARY***

Grammar

- **Syntax and accidence:** (not family members; members of a family)

- **Usage:** Roots, branches, fruits etc. (Enthusiasm: *En* within+ *theos* 'god'= power to create! The *Brahma* aspect.
- **Words:** Distinctions and Misapplication.
- **Balance vocabulary:** Catch phrase: Jargon: price wise, client wise.
- **Voice:** It is the thought behind the words which gives them power, not superficial oratory. So your aim at the start is to be typical of yourself. You must endeavour to reveal your true personality when you speak, suiting your voice with appropriate vocabulary-and getting an individual angle on the subject.

Stance: Stand upright, legs slightly apart, hands across the chest, palms downwards and fingertips touching, elbows slightly below the shoulder line.

Clarity of Diction: Every word must be enunciated according to its importance, some with more emphasis than the others, but ALL must be heard.

Tone and Pitch: We all possess a natural middle tone. Some of us have higher pitched voices than others with different middle registers, so do not try and change this.

Timing: In this sense timing is not our speech length in minutes but how you deliver your material. It is involved with pausing and correct emphasis.

Ums and Ers: Be careful of unnecessary *Ums* and *Ers*.

Material and forms of speech making: Never be a one speech maker. Widen your material. Train your mind to absorb speech material. Memory is a matter of paying attention; It is in itself a filling system. You must be a good mixture. Harvest material all you can.

Time: Keep to your allotted time. Don't get carried away. Always leave your audience wanting more but never give it to them.

Meiosis: This is a disease like name droppers: speaking of a car accident after dinner with Miss Right.

Speech and Structure: Like a short story must have a beginning, middle and end.

Sentences: Vary them.

Loose: My name is Bond

Periodic: Bond is my name

Balance: Many tried; **few** were successful

Seven ways to be a good conversationalist
• Be interested
• Be friendly
• Be cheerful, good humoured
• Be animated, yet relaxed
• Be flexible
• Be tactful
• Be courteous

Eight Don't's in conversation
• Don't be dogmatic
• Don't be condescending
• Don't be argumentative
• Don't be lifeless
• Don't be insincere
• Don't be egocentric

- Don't be aimed to be the life of a party
- Don't be a mumbler

Seven faults in conversation

- Pet words: fabulous, tremendous,
- Superfluous words and phrases: Naturally, actually, literally
- Fad words: overall picture, contact, dynamic
- Too much slang: yup, guys
- Affectations: too much of foreign words; bete noire, amour
- Exaggerating: The funniest story I ever heard
- Telling personal experiences awkwardly

Five ways to say NO

- Put it on an impersonal basis
- Make it clear that you would like to say 'Yes'
- Say 'No' by helping the person say 'No' to himself.
- In saying 'No', show what needs to be done to get a 'Yes'
- Most important, say your 'No' in the nicest, warmest way you can

PRESENTATION (FEEDBACK)	
NAME	:
POSTURE AND STANCE	:
CLARITY AND DICTION	:
AUDIBILITY	
TONE AND PITCH	:
EYE CONTACT	:
FACIAL	
BODY LANGUAGE	:
GESTURES	
PRESENTATION	:
3 Vs ASSESSMENT	
Verbal	:
Vocal	:
Visual	:
OTHER REMARKS	:

CUE CARD		
INTRODUCTION	:	Beginning
BODY	:	Middle
CONCLUSION	:	End
BEGINNING PROTOCOL	:	
ENDING PROTOCOL	:	

How to Introduce a Speaker

The basic functions to introduce a speaker are three:
- to dispose the audience favourably towards the speaker
- to underline the importance or relevance of the topic in question
- to indicate the credentials and competence of the speaker in this regard.

Obviously, much will depend on circumstances but here are some tips:

- Familiarize yourself with the speaker's background. Do not read from his bio-data sheet unless absolutely necessary. Pronounce his are her name correctly.(Or else as David Daiches the literary critic once retorted when his name was often mispronounced: "You are not righteous when you cannot pronounce DAVID *Daie-chez"*

- Be cheerful, warm, and enthusiastic. This is contagious.

- Avoid the commonplace; e.g. 'for having graced this occasion by taking time out of his busy schedule.'

- Be accurate. Don't have the speaker wondering who is being introduced.

- Often it is effective to single out *one quality* or accomplishment or the speaker rather than give an undifferentiated litany of their past. Sometimes the method of 'passing over' is helpful.

TIS: Introducing a speaker
• T : Topic
• I : Importance of Topic
• S : Speaker

Note: Don't turn to look at the speaker while introducing him/her. Your voice will be taken away from the microphone.

Give a Vote of Thanks

A vote of thanks should be like a punctuation mark at the end of a sentence: a full stop, a question or exclamation mark. The average speech calls only for a full stop; a scintillating one for a an exclamation mark, while a controversial or tendentious talk may require a question mark. In every case, however, the vote of thanks should be *brief*.

Tips for your vote of thanks:
• Be relevant
• Refer to the central thought or position that struck you most.
• Be positive
• This is no time for nit-picking or display of your analytical skills. Emphasize the positive, forget about the negative.
• Be crisp
• Most speakers go beyond their time. The audience is frequently tired. You're just a punctuation mark. Don't try to be a sentence – or even worse, a paragraph. Be brief and be gone.
A vote of thanks, then, should add something, i.e. make a positive contribution to the occasion. One of the best vote of thanks that one can expect consists of ten words: "Mr Mehra, for the best evening we've had in ages, thank you."

The 5 Canons of Persuasive Presentations

It may be a new process, product, or project that the school, industry or organization should embrace but all of us should be able to put across a proposal effectively within a limited period of time.

I. Purpose:	Be absolutely clear about your purpose. You should be able to state in one clear sentence what you wish to accomplish. The objective of your presentation may not be the same as the objective of your proposal.
II. Preparation:	1. Research your audience (individuals or organization) thoroughly. What problems, needs do they have related to your proposal? Who are the decision makers? How open-minded are they likely to be? 2. Know exactly how much time you will be given: plan it for input, audio-visuals, questions and answers. 3. See the room where you will make the presentation. Where will you stand? Will you need a microphone? 4. Have your equipment ready to run: e.g., charts, transparencies and slides checked for proper order; projector, tape recorder and the LCD at the desired volume and focus, all preset, tested and adjusted, needing only a 'switch on' to run.

III. Problem:	Your introduction needs to grab the audience's attention. It must answer the question: "why should I listen?" Make your listeners identify with you through your solid knowledge of their situation and needs. Show the gap between what is and what could be. Have a clear structure for your message and repeat it: the organization of your remarks largely determines how much of your message will be retained.
IV. Possibilities:	Name and evaluate the alternative ways of closing the gap between actual and ideal.
V. Proposal:	With enthusiasm, show how your proposal- meets their needs better than any other possibility. Handle questions pleasantly. Close exactly on time.

How to Argue a Case

It may be just a debate. It may be a land dispute or a case before a labour court, tribunal or arbitrator. At any rate, the ability to argue a case effectively is a skill we all develop. Here are some tips:

1. *Prepare the case for the other party before you prepare your own.* Preparing the strongest possible case for the other party is the best way to anticipate and foresee the other party's strategy and strong points.
2. Be sure of your facts.

a. What are the facts admitted by both sides; the 'facts' admitted only by one side; the 'facts' admitted by neither?
   b. Distinguish clearly the facts, interpretation of facts (conjecture, opinion), and hearsay.
   c. What assumption are you making? What assumptions may the other party make?
3. *In legal cases, argue from the definition.* The important point is not how we define a term, nor how other people define it, but how does the law define it. The legal definition is crucial and often different from ordinary usage.
4. *Know the leading cases.* Know both those that favour your position and those that don't. Also what was the precise point of emphasis in each, and what was secondary or said only in passing?
5. *Marshall your arguments.* After you have examined the facts, prepared the opposition's case, familiarize yourself with the key definitions and leading cases, you are ready to prepare your own case. What are your strong points and weak points and in what order will you present them?

Speaking Goal

Getting on your feet before an audience always means a little risk. Take calculated risks, i.e. risks that have at least 50% probability of succeeding. Make sure, however, that there's always a little stretch in your targets.

The ability to put your thoughts across persuasively to groups is a skill that helps in many ways.

Write one speaking goal that you are setting for yourself

for the next few months. After writing the goal in the box below, assess it for **Importance (I)** and **Difficulty (D)**, Also check to see whether there is any **conflict** with any other goal of yours **(C)**.

Speaking goal for the next few months	I	D	C

Rudiments of Public Speaking Charms
Don't Try to be a Public Speaker!

'Charm' is a way of getting the answer 'yes' without having asked any clear question wrote Albert Camus. That is the 'magic' of public speaking!

Public speaking is enlarged conversation. There is little difference between speaking to one person, or a hundred persons. You must talk louder; but the talking that goes on in your drawing room or dinner table does not differ in essence from the talking that goes on at a meeting. The only difference is that at a meeting the speaker is allowed to talk for a longer time without interruptions.

Therefore, we ought to think of our speech as a conversation with the audience. The bottom line of public speaking is emphatic: Talk *with* the persons you see in front of you. Talk *to* them. But never ever, never talk *at* them.

The structure of your speech should be discussion driven. Think of it as a discussion with people you know. Imagine they have asked you an important question and you are doing your best to answer. As you do, they put other questions to you, and you try to answer these. You explain, tell stories to illustrate what you mean, and cite statistics. Finally, you sum up everything you've said with a "There's that it. That's what I've been saying."

If you think of and prepare your address in these ways, it will be *good talking*.

Public speaking is purposeful communication. You talk to an audience for a purpose. You want them to feel, think, to do something. Therefore, during your speech, concentrate on this objective. Keep your eye on the ball. Keep your focus clear and vivid.

- Don't fall a victim to distractions by latecomers or noises.
- Don't let you talking become mechanical. If you let your attention wander, your manner will become absentminded and you will not communicate.
- Think what you are saying while you are saying it. Think it hard.

Then the audience will know that you mean what you say and will listen to you.

PROFILE OF A GOOD SPEAKER

- A good speaker is lively, interested, enthusiastic and vital. He feels alive; he sees his audience as living people. He is interested in his topic and considers it vital to such people. So he speaks of it with enthusiasm. That's the best way to interest an audience.
- A good speaker is earnest. He doesn't talk for talk's sake, to show off his clothes, or his smile, or his diction, or his voice. He doesn't turn on the charm when he stands up only to switch it off as he sits down.

- A good speaker has a sense of responsibility to his listeners. He realizes that if he talks for five minutes to a hundred listeners he is taking five hundred minutes out of people's lives. He tries to say something that will be worth that precious time.
- A good speaker has a sense of responsibility to others on the program. If he has allotted five minutes, he does not take ten. He takes care not to squeeze others off the program, or force them to hurry. They, too, may have something worthwhile to say.
- A good speaker has a sense of responsibility to his subject. He doesn't bite off more than he can chew. He doesn't spread it thin.
- A good speaker has a sense of leadership: he stands up tall; he talks eye to eye; he speaks responsibly and with authority, as a leader should. He is positive, friendly, and straightforward.
- A good speaker keeps his head. He doesn't let his enthusiasm carry him too far. He doesn't let his confidence become overconfidence. He doesn't let himself get intoxicated with the sense of power that comes with being in the public eye.
- A good speaker tries to be balanced.
- A good speaker keeps his sense of humor.

From the beginning speaker: Be yourself. Say what you think, not what some columnist or newscaster thinks.

Study other speakers, but don't ape them.

Recognize and admire the fine qualities you must have. Work out your own style; discover what will make you an effective speaker.

Therefore, the key to the beginning speaker: know yourself.

Do not indulge in wishful thinking about your speaking ability. Be realistic about the extent of your capabilities.

Learn to accept criticism and to profit by it.

After each performance, analyze it. Try to form some objective estimate of its worth.

Discover the weaknesses; don't cover them up. Do something to correct them.

Discover your strengths. Emphasize them and develop them.

The Organized Public Speaker – You – The How, What, and Why of Public Speaking

Groom Yourself as a Public Speaker

The shakers and movers of this world are the men and women who convincingly get their ideas across to others. Seldom do people accomplish anything alone. People must communicate to eliminate the generation gaps, the cultural gaps, or the economic gaps.

When you master the art of making a good speech, presenting it with poise and charm or charisma, you will learn many things that will remain your lifelong assets. You will learn much about yourself and your best style of presentation. You will learn how to research and organize the facts about a topic and how to evaluate them in terms of significance and of importance to various audiences.

Though winning gives us a thrill...of greater importance is the trying, the learning, and the knowledge gained. How effectively you communicate throughout your life will reflect in your home, your work, your community, and even your country.

How You Feel Communicates Itself to the Audience

How you look, how much you know about your subject, and how much you care about persuading your audience will affect your presentation.

How You Look

Get enough rest before your appearance, and eat sparingly. Wear attractive but comfortable clothing in which you are at ease. Good grooming is well worth the small investment of extra time it takes to help you make your best appearance. Relax, smile, and take a deep breath before you begin. Look as if you're glad to be there! Establish eye contact constantly with all members of your audience. Use "body language"... natural, unaffected actions and gestures to punctuate the points you wish to emphasize.

What do You Know About it?

If you're interested in your topic, your audience will be too; therefore, choose a topic that interests you so everything you learn about it will have extra meaning for you.

Keep your **posture** erect but not stiff. You have often seen nervous speakers grip the mike, lean into it or lean away from it. Check out the public address system in advance and determine by testing the best distance from the mike, then speak into it. Some mikes are affected by metallic objects such as rings or watches coming too close to them; this is another potential disturbance factor you can check out in advance.

Mike fright or stage fright attacks the amateur *and* the seasoned performer at times. If you are nervous, breathe deeply and slowly several times just before you are introduced...or consciously relax your body, arms, and legs as much as possible. Stand erect, and walk briskly to the lectern. Try to appear confident, and speak loudly enough to be heard well throughout the room. If you smile often and communicate your friendliness, your audience probably will root for you.

Your speech will have three main parts...the **introduction**, in which you greet and warm up your audience, then stimulate their appetites for what you are about to tell them; secondly, the **body of the speech**, which is the main portion of your talk. Try not to have more than three to five main points; more might confuse you and your audience. The **conclusion** presents a brief summary of your main points. And you may find it effective to close on a high note with a poem, quotation, joke, surprise statement or challenge and, of course, a warm compliment to the audience.

I. Introduction
  A. Opening
     - Personal anecdote **or**
     - Startling statement of fact **or**
     - Quote **or**
     - Poem **or**
     - Appropriate joke or story
  B. Preview—Tell your audience (in capsule form) what you are going to cover in your talk

II. Body
  A. The "meat and potatoes" of your public speaking assignment
     - Speech patterns
     - Past...present...future—in other words—problems...damage...solution
     - Cause...effect...action needed

III. Conclusion
- Summary
- Closing—Appeal for action from your audience (give, join, support, volunteer)

Once you've written your outline, read it to a friend or family member...or, if you can, try it out several ways on a cassette recorder/player. Check your presentation for its sequence, its transition, the logic of the central thought, the persuasiveness of your arguments, and the responses you want from your potential audiences. Make any necessary revisions to achieve your objective...that of communicating your **big idea!**

If you have the material well in mind, you may want to transfer your outline of the speech to 3 by 5 index cards. Knowing you have help close at hand will give you extra confidence. (Cards don't rattle, as papers frequently do, if your hands should shake a time or two.)

Act confidently, even if you don't feel that way, and the next thing you know you will be self-assured. Practice makes perfect. Your ability to clarify your thoughts and ideas and your ability to influence others will steadily improve with each public speaking engagement. Your confidence will grow, and you will learn to anticipate audience response to your planned pauses or whatever devices you use to keep your speech well-paced.

Your public speaking successes are based on the content of your talk and the delivery and its effect on the audience. Try rating yourself on the organization of your speech, your voice (variance of pitch and volume to avoid monotony), pronunciation, enunciation, grammar, timing, and use of notes.

The fuses may blow, the soup may spill, or a prop may

drop or fail to work. Hundreds of so-called mishaps have happened to other speakers in other settings...and the quick-witted speaker will often turn the minor or real disaster to advantage. **Do not panic**...keep thinking, and you may become a "legend in your own time."

In more ways than one, certainly, it's your time to shine... but don't forget to be courteous to the chairperson, the other speakers, the sponsors, and the audience. They want to like you and they will, if you keep their needs in mind. They want to be informed, inspired, and entertained...and you're there to do just that—not to go on an ego trip.

Hold up your head. Have your notes high enough for easy reading, but be sure you can see your audience and they can see you over the notes. Your eyes are also as important as your voice. Keep looking at the audience as much as possible. The floor and the ceiling are not views for your eyes! Even your notes merit your eyes as little as possible.

Your voice is **you** on this occasion. It must be heard, so don't let it be too low or too soft; on the other hand, don't let it become too loud. Speak distinctly and moderately fast. Think about what you are saying; stick to the time limits. Most people give their full attention for about 20 minutes. If you must speak longer, allow for a break on occasion and then repeat.

Check your mannerisms for things that may destroy your effectiveness. Don't repeat "and uh." Don't twirl your pen and pencil, twist your tie or your coat or jacket buttons, grip the podium as if it is supporting you, rub the back of your neck, or do any of the many things speakers sometimes do unconsciously when too absorbed in thoughts. People forget the impressions they might be projecting to others.

Technical subjects are often easier to communicate when you use audio or visual aids. Demonstrations with commonplace materials may help your audience understand a process, and the "props" might grab their attention. Listed are some visual aids to consider in making your public speaking presentation.

- **Flannel, magnet, or loop board**—use letters 1 to 2 inches high, ¼ of an inch thick; use graphics easily seen and understood from a distance of 30 to 40 feet.
- **Chalk board**—lettering 1½ to 2 inches high and as thick as can be made with soft white chalk.
- **Easel pad, flip charts**—letters 1½ to 2 inches high, ¼ of an inch thick; use graphics easily readable from 30 to 40 feet.

These suggested visual aids are best for talks and demonstrations for groups of 35 or fewer.

- **Photographs**—8 by 10 or larger with matte finish. Exhibit where the audience can get close.
- **Slides**—keep lettering to 5 lines, 15 to 20 letters per line on original. Use close-up with long and medium shots for real thing.
- **Overhead transparency**—keep lettering ½ of an inch high on the transparency. Use in talks for medium-sized groups.
- **Video**—keep lettering to 5 lines, 15 to 20 letters per line on original. Use close-up with long and medium shots of real thing. Use in talks and demonstrations for larger groups.
- **Real things or models**—some visual aids have limited use due to variations in size. Check each usage. Talks and demonstrations for small groups.

Introductions
Introduce the speaker by first and last name and give an overview of the speaker's affiliation. Tell where he/she came from and where he/she lives. Briefly, tell the qualifications relating to the subject as well as any unusual fact that might get the audience's attention. Give the topic to be presented to the audience; provide a brief statement that will give the audience a sense of anticipation.

Presentations
Tell why the honor/award is being presented, by whom it is being awarded, and the basis on which the honoree was selected. Mention other specific accomplishments of the honoree and the influence this person's actions has on others. Build anticipation for the presentation, then announce the honoree. Present the award, congratulate the recipient, and step away from the podium or microphone so the recipient may acknowledge the presentation. Do not comment on the recipient's speech, mannerisms, or appearance, even jokingly. Emphasize the symbolic and inspirational meaning of the award or gift!

Acceptance
Appreciation is the keynote of an acceptance speech. Thank the person presenting the gift, the honor, or donor organization. Express gratitude to those who helped you win the award or those who placed you in position to achieve it. Express your regard for the significance of the award and for the responsibility it places on you to continue to live up to it. Express your thanks again briefly in closing.

Extemporaneous Speeches
Whether predictable or unpredictable, the extemporaneous speech is delivered in the same manner as a prepared speech, except you probably will want to confine yourself

to one main idea or point. Often you can use what someone else has just said as a takeoff point, immediately identifying you with the audience. **Remember.** You are "never totally unprepared." All of your life experiences can prepare you for this moment. By being natural, relying on your own or your friends' experiences, or connecting the occasion with your current reading, TV viewing, or radio listening, you always have a wealth of "material" at the tip of your tongue.

Reports

Committe reports are usually limited to 3 minutes according to the bylaws of many organizations. Still, more brief reports are in order if the meeting's agenda is lengthy. Present your complete reports in writing; distribute the report after you have read it to the group. (Distributing the report before you speak gives your audience an opportunity to read it instead of listening to you!)

Sample Openings

A personal narrative is a good opening for a speech. A relevant story helps establish a common ground between your subject and your audience. For example, throughout the year, major televised events provide general interest to a wide range of audiences.

Your opening comments could include a statement such as the following: "Last week as I watched the final game of the World Cup, I noted the stands packed with avid fans. Millions of individuals like myself were watching the game on TV, and I thought, 'how wonderful it would be if as much attention could be brought to the subject I am to present to you today."

A startling statement can capture the audience's attention.

A quote is effective. An appropriate joke or story can capture your audience's attention quickly.

"Before I say 'good-bye' to you today, I have a few stories and comments to share. I am here to talk to you on the subject of _____."

Closing With a Quote

For example: "I would like to leave you this thought expressed by Descartes: 'I think, therefore I AM'."

Boring Speeches—The Ten Deadly Sins

The TEN Commandments is a number that could also be associated with the TEN deadly sins of Boring speeches.

In public speaking all of the sins count. We have listened to some awfully boring speeches. Indeed, come to think of it, some of us have given a few ourselves. Perhaps each one of us is a perfect expert to be the judge of the World's Most Boring Lecture Competition.

What makes a truly boring public speech? Ten skills can be deployed. Alas, on exquisite occasions, all of them are present in ghastly combination.

1. A boring topic

- Political interpretations of a joke about bananas.
- The Etymological differences of left from right.
- A post-structural analysis of Shakespeare's poetry (with translations into Hindi).

If one hangs around long enough in the public speaking circuit, one can accomplish much and quite easily fall into the first sin. "Cyber Crime Substitutes and the Law". Perhaps the audience may ask this question: Is there nothing you will not speak about?"

But at least Cyber Crime substitutes may be enlivened by occasional references to MMS morphing of celebrity women. It is almost impossible to give a talk on romance and to make it boring. Yet some have succeeded.

2. Boring length

There are some public speakers, many of them politicians and some judges, who are accomplished experts in this second sin. Krishna Menon could speak at the UN for just about 12 hours. Fidel Castro can speak for hours, without drawing breath. In the old days of the Soviet Union, the speeches of members of the Politbureau were faithfully recorded in all their magnificent duration. The only relief arose from interruptions, recorded as "applause", "prolonged applause" and "thunderous prolonged applause". Physical activity such as leaping to one's feet and moving arms and hands together in frenzies motion, can be a safe, but temporary, way of keeping awake.

Boring length is not at all difficult for many public speakers. Some spoil-sports ruin everything by unseemly brevity. Winston Churchill, invited to return to Harrow, his old school, was asked at the last minute to say something to the boys. He rose and all that he said was: "Never give up. Never give up. Never give up". This said it all. But it could have been eked out for several hours, a hymn to a boring length.

3. Boring jokes

There is plenty of humor about boredom itself. Most of it is suitably boring.
- Herbert Beerbohn Tree reportedly described a friend as "An old bore. Even the grave yawns for him";

- John Updike wrote an essay which he modestly called "Confessions of a Wild Bore". In it he declared that "a healthy male adult bore consumes each year one and a half times his own weight in other people's patience".
- Oscar Wilde, who should have known, declared in *A Woman of No Importance* that to be in society was "merely a bore". But to be out of it was "simply a tragedy".

A boring public speaker must never use humor to telling effect.

4. Boring confusion

It is interesting to be part of a glazed eye audience watching as such a speaker ambles to a much prayed-for ending. Waiting for that magic word, "Finally". Wondering where on earth the talk is going. Fearing that it is irretrievably lost in dense undergrowth. Hoping against hope that the agony will soon be over. Even more interesting is the fate of looking at an audience as they exhibit these emotions - and wondering to one's self when (if at all) one's speech will be over.

To announce concisely the objectives of a speech is an anathema to them. To display a structure - beginning, middle and end - is alien to their nature. Those spoilsports who do so have no chance of committing the fourth sin.

5. Boring language

Recent studies of why the German people enjoy a tendency to melancholia have begun to concentrate on their language. How would you like to spend a lifetime contorting face and tongue into the peculiarities of the Umlaut? Anyone in doubt should attend a conference of public speakers in Germany. Some languages are joyous and playful, as Italian seems to be. English with its hisses and th's and sylabet sounds, so difficult for envious foreigners, happily portrays much of its Germanic origins.

6. Boring self-absorption

Everyone has his or her little obsession. In Australia and India, it usually takes the form of a football or cricket team. With a little persistence, a public speaker with such obsessions is well on the way to a first class honors degree in boredom.

7. Boring clichés

Public discourse is full of boring clichés. Sometimes they come in the form of political correctness. Those guilty of expressing them will be slapped down by journalistic scribes. Such speakers deserve such rebukes. They have forgotten the seventh deadly sin.

8. Boring delivery

Those who really work at this sin can do wonders. It takes a special skill to speak for an hour or more at a single pitch and tone. Yet quite a few are highly accomplished at this art. Many regard microphones as things to be defied, to be left disengaged or to be totally ignored during delivery.

One particularly skilful way of securing top marks on this eighth sin is to read a speech written by others. Unless a speech writer is familiar with the language and verbal patterns of a speaker, he or she can wreak havoc on the speaker's delivery. Remember the film '3 Idiots'!

9. Boring inflexibility

It was not this way in the days of radio. A few like Churchill had a command of pause. Radio is somehow more conducive to content than television is. Nowadays, if a public speaker pauses for effect, or to let an important idea sink in, he or she is likely to be zapped. The medium is truly the message. It is designed for a very visual generation, with a low average IQ and an even lower attention span.

Imagery now is everything. The choice of the most important elected public official in the world, the Political leader turns less and less on the content of the candidates' public speeches. It turns more and more on a prolonged pumping hands, namastes, and on analysis of sighs, eye gestures and apparent personal charm. A former Prime Minister goes down in the polls for sighing once too often and rolling his eyes. He possibly did this to keep himself awake. Some politicians goes up because he seems a nice kind of guy whom you would be prepared, reluctantly, to have to dinner.

Welcome to the world in which the new media nurtures new forms of boredom. The speaker who is bereft without his slides. The lecturer who always puts her transparencies upside down. The laptop that brings every international conference to a grinding halt because it simply refuses to deliver the visuals designed to add dazzle and glitz to a speaker.

10. Boring peoples' rights

Perhaps boredom is genetic. People simply cannot help it. Indeed, the gene probably manifests itself in two types: borers and borees.

Some of those who yawn and fall asleep are not even reacting to one's cultivated witticisms and entrancing thoughts. They are simply physiological victims of sleep apnoea. All they need is to attach themselves to a machine. If they do not snore at night, they will not sleep through public addresses. Pity them. They are victims.

NEVER try to recall what you had written and rehearsed. Speak as it comes to you naturally. It will be far superior than the write up.

Impromptu Speaking

There are times when we are asked to get up and say a few words about someone or a topic when we have not planned on saying anything at all. We are more shocked than anyone else. Has this ever happened to you? If and when this does happen to you, be prepared to rise to the challenge.

Some tips

- Decide quickly what your one message will be - Keep in mind you have not been asked to give a speech but to make some impromptu remarks. Pick ONE message or comment and focus on that one main idea. Many times, other ideas may come to you after you start speaking. If this happens, go with the flow and trust your instincts.
- Do not try and memorize what you will say - Trying to memorize will only make you more nervous and you will find yourself thinking more about the words and not about the message.
- Start off strong and with confidence - If you at least plan your opening statement, this will get you started on the right foot. Getting started is the most difficult. Plan what your first sentence will be. If you know you have three points or ideas to say, just start off simple by saying, "I would just like to talk about 3 points".

The first point is... the second point is... and so on. This keeps you within your desired ambit.

- Decide on your transitions from one point to the other - After you have decided on your opening remark or line, come up with a simple transition statement that takes you to your main point. If you have more than one point to make, you can use a natural transition such as, "My second point is... or my next point is..." etc. Just list your points. Do not write out the exact words, but just the points you want to mention.
- Maintain eye contact with the audience - This is easier to do if you do not have a written script. Maintain eye contact with your audience and speak from your heart. Focus on communicating TO your audience and not speaking AT the crowd.
- Occasionally throw in an off-the-cuff remark - Because you want your style to be flexible and seem impromptu, trust your instinct and add a few words which just pop into your head. Keep it conversational and think of the audience as a group of your friends.
- Finally, have a good conclusion - "And the last point I would like to make is ...". Once you have made your last point, you can then turn control back to the person who asked you to speak in the first place.

With a little practice, this process will feel more natural to you. Anticipating that you MAY be asked to say a few words should force you to at least think about what you might say if you are asked. Then if you ARE asked, you are better prepared because you anticipated being asked. This is much better than thinking they won't ask you and they actually do!

Gestures

Gestures are reflections of every speaker's individual personality. What's right for one speaker may not be right for another. **Six rules** apply to anyone who seeks to become a dynamic effective speaker.

1. **Respond naturally to what you think, feel, and see**
   It's natural for you to gesture, and it's unnatural for you not to. If you inhibit your impulse to gesture, you will probably become tense.

2. **Create the condition for gesturing, not the gesture**
   When you speak, you should be totally involved in communicating - not thinking about your hands. Your gestures should be motivated by the content of your presentation.

3. **Suit the action to the word and the occasion**
   Your visual and verbal messages must function as partners in communicating the same thought or feeling. Every gesture you make should be purposeful and reflective of your words so the audience will note only the effect, not the gesture itself. Don't overdo the gesturing. You'll draw the listener away from your message. Young audiences are usually attracted to a speaker who uses vigorous gestures, but older, more conservative groups may feel irritated or threatened by a speaker whose physical actions are overwhelming.

4. **Make your gestures convincing**
   Your gestures should be lively and distinct if they are to convey the intended impressions. Effective gestures are vigorous enough to be convincing yet slow enough and broad enough to be clearly visible without being overpowering.

5. Make your gestures smooth and well timed

Every gesture has three parts:
- **The Approach** - Your body begins to move in anticipation.
- **The Stroke** - The gesture itself.
- **The Return** - This brings your body back to a balanced posture.

The flow of a gesture - the approach, the stroke, the return-must be smoothly executed so that only the stroke is evident to the audience. While it is advisable to practice gesturing, don't try to memorize your every move. This makes your gesturing stilted and ineffective.

6. Make natural, spontaneous gesturing a habit

The first step in becoming adept at gesturing is to determine what, if anything, you are doing now.

To improve gestures, practice - but never during a speech. Practice gesturing while speaking informally to friends, family member, and co-workers.

LCD Display Projectors - Tips

1. **Read the LCD projector manual on its proper operation** Not all LCD projectors work the same and each has its own unique operating requirements. Become very familiar with the projector BEFORE using it during your actual presentation. Make sure your computer can be properly interfaced with the LCD projector.

2. **Practice setting the equipment up several times** Spend some time making sure you know how to properly set up the LCD projector with your computer and other computers. Set up the LCD projector in the actual presentation environment you will be using, if possible.

3. **Set up well in advance** Allow yourself plenty of time to set up your computer and the LCD projector. Check any last minute details.
4. **Check the LCD projector bulb life** LCD projector bulbs do have limited life. Some bulbs have shorter lives than others. Check and make sure the bulb you will be using is not close to the end of its life.
5. **Bring a spare bulb and cables!** Always carry spare bulbs with you and make sure you know how to properly change the bulb. Also, remember, "Hot" glass looks like "Cold" glass; be careful and bring a towel or glove to use when changing the bulb. Practice changing the bulb during one of your practice sessions.
6. **Check your presentation color combinations** Take some time to check out the actual presentation for the color combinations you will be using. Some colors and color combinations do not project well.
7. **Check the font size you are using** Nothing is more frustrating to an audience than text that cannot be easily seen or read. Make sure you are using the proper text size for the distance you will be projecting your slides.

Many presentations today are followed up with a question and answer period. To some people this can be the most exciting part of the presentation. To others it can be their worst nightmare. In fact, there are some presenters who purposely avoid the question and answer period all together.

Handling Questions: 5 Steps

1. **Listen to the entire question** Listen to the entire question BEFORE you begin to answer any questions.

Too many people start responding to a question before the entire question is even asked. Not waiting to hear the entire questions can result in you providing a response which had nothing to do with the question. Force yourself to LISTEN to the entire question and make sure you understand the question.

2. **Pause** and allow yourself time to value the question and listener. REPEAT the question out loud so the entire audience can hear it. It is important that everyone "hear" the question or the answer you provide may not make sense to some of the people. By repeating the question, this will allow you some additional time to evaluate the question and formulate a response.

3. **Credit the Person** for asking the question. You may say something like, "That was a great question" or, "Glad you asked that question". One word of caution. If you credit one person with asking a question, be sure to credit EVERYONE for asking a question. You don't want people to feel their question was not as important.

4. **Respond to the Question** honestly and the best you can. If you do NOT know an answer to a question, do not try to fake it. Be honest, and tell them you do not know but DO promise to research the answer for them and DO get back to them.

5. **Bridge** to the next question by asking them a question. "Does that answer your question?", "Is that the kind of information you were looking for?" This is critical. Once they respond to you, "YES" you now have permission to go on to the next person. This also gives them one more opportunity to say, "No" and allow them to clarify their question more by asking it again.

Handling Questions: Additional Tips

I. Ask people to stand up when they ask a question. This does two things: (1) It shows you more readily who is asking the question, and (2) It makes it easier for the audience to also hear the question.

II. Have small sheets of paper available for people to write down their questions during your presentation. They may forget what they were going to ask earlier.

III. Allow people to pass the questions to you if they feel uncomfortable standing up and asking the question out loud. This gives the person who truly wants to ask a question an option.

IV. Always repeat the question - this does three things: (1) it makes sure you understood the question, (2) it gives you a chance to value the question and think of an answer, and (3) it assures the other people in the audience can hear the question since you are facing them.

V. Always take time to think "before" you answer all questions. This allows you time to think, especially for those difficult questions. Do the same for those questions you readily know the answer for. Responding too quickly to those questions you are most comfortable with will only bring attention to those questions you do not.

VI. Jot down or write down questions you can't answer. This way, you can properly follow up with the person who asked the question you couldn't answer. Be sure to get their name and phone number or address. Promise to get back to them and DO get back to them.

Preparing and Delivering Presentations: 7 Aspects

An effective speaker learns to deal with all **7 aspects** at the same time. Failure to pay attention to all of these aspects can result in an ineffective presentation. Failure to pay attention to too many of these can result in disaster.

1. Speaker
2. Message
3. Audience
4. Channel
5. Feedback
6. Noise
7. Setting

ASPECT 1 - The Speaker

One of the major components of any speech or presentation is the speaker themselves. Many people forget that THEY are the presentation and NOT the visual aids. Many presenters today put so much effort into the visual aids; they forget that those are just aids to the speaker.

There are *three factors* we need to consider about any speaker:

a. His/Her motivation in giving the presentation
b. His/Her credibility as a speaker
c. His/Her delivery or speaking style

a. A Speaker's motivation can be approached in terms of two considerations:
- Whether direct personal reward (e.g. Rupees) or indirect rewards (feeling good about helping others) are involved.

- Whether immediate rewards (Rupees today) or delayed rewards (getting a college degree after 4 years of college play a part.)

  In essence, a speaker may be motivated by one or BOTH of these factors. Before speaking you should consider what YOUR motivations are.

b. Speaker's credibility

   A speaker's ideas are accepted as believable only to the degree that the speaker is perceived to be credible. The speaker's credibility depends on his or her trustworthiness, competence, and good will. The speaker who is well organized will usually be considered competent. The speaker who is attractive and dynamic will be seen as more credible than one who is not.

   The most fundamental factor a speaker projects is the attitude they have toward himself.

c. Speaker's delivery

   The delivery, the way the message is presented, should compliment the speech's objective. A well written speech delivered poorly can quickly lose effectiveness.

ASPECT 2 - The Message

The message refers to EVERYTHING a speaker does or says, both verbally and non-verbally. The verbal part may be analyzed in terms of 3 basic elements:

- Content
- Style
- Structure

a. **Content** - is what you say about your topic. The content is the MEAT of your speech or presentation. Research your topic thoroughly. Decide on how much to say about each subject. Then decide on the actual sequence you will use. It is important that you consider the audience's needs, time factors, and other items as the content of your speech or presentation is prepared and presented

b. **Style** - The manner in which you present the content of your speech is your style. Styles can vary from very formal to the very informal. Most presentations fall between these two extremes and in EVERY case, the style should be determined by what is appropriate to the speaker, the audience, as well as the occasion and setting.

c. **Structure** - The structure of a message is its organization. There are many organizational variations, but in each case, the structure should include:
  - An Introduction
  - A Body
  - A Conclusion

The **introduction** should include:
- an opening attention grabber such as a quote or shocking statistic
- an agenda
- the purpose or main message of your presentation

The **body** should include:
- the main points or ideas
- points which support the main message

The **conclusion** should include:
- a summary of your main points
- a closing grabber
- time for questions and answers, if appropriate

When speeches and presentations are poorly organized, the impact of the message is reduced and the audience is less likely to accept the speaker or the speaker's ideas.

ASPECT 3 - The Audience

As a speaker you should analyze your listeners and then decide how to present your ideas. This analysis might include considerations related to:

- Age
- Sex
- Marital Status
- Geographic location
- Group membership
- Education
- Career

For example, if you are making a presentation on "Future Careers", knowing your audience's average age is vital. A well prepared speech that is ill-suited to the audience can have the same effect as a poorly prepared speech delivered to the correct audience. Both speeches will fail terribly.

Proper audience analysis will assure that you give the right speech to the right audience. To properly customize the speech, most professional speakers send their clients a multi-page questionnaire in order to gather information about them and their speaking event.

Using the word "A-U-D-I-E-N-C-E" as an acronym: general audience analysis categories that your surveys should include:

A_udience	- Who are the members? How many will be at the event?
U_nderstanding	- What is their knowledge about the topic you will be addressing?
D_emographics	- What is their age, sex, educational background, etc.?
I_nterest	- Why will they be at this event? Who asked them to be there?
E_nvironment	- Where will I stand when I speak? Will everyone be able to see me?
N_eeds	- What are the listener's needs? What are your needs as a speaker? What are the needs of the person who hired you?
C_ustomized	- How can I custom fit my message to this audience?
E_xpectations	- What do the listeners expect to learn from me?

ASPECT 4 - The Channel

When we communicate with our audiences, we use many channels of communication. This includes non-verbal, pictorial and aural channels.

It is very important that you use as many channels as you can to communicate with your audience. The more channels of communication you can use at the same time, the better. Basically there are **three** channels:

A. Nonverbal
1. gestures
2. facial expressions
3. body movement

4. posture

B. Pictorial
1. diagrams
2. charts
3. graphs
4. pictures
5. objects

C. Aural
1. tone of your voice
2. variations in pitch and volume
3. other vocal variety

ASPECT 5 - The Feedback

"Feedback" is the process through which the speaker receives information about how his or her message has been received by the listeners and, in turn, responds to those cues.

The feedback process is not complete until the speaker has responded to the listener. This process includes the listener's reactions to the speaker's response.

One can ask your audience questions and even ask them what their understanding is of the point you have just made. Watch for non-verbal clues from your audience and be prepared to respond to the reactions of your audience throughout your presentation.

It is the speaker's responsibility to provide the information the audience needs to hear. Many times, you may be asked by management to provide a specific message to their employees that they may not want to hear. Remember, it is the management that is paying your fee and you are responsible to deliver the message they hired you to deliver. At the same time, it is important that you are sensitive to the audience and try to establish a relationship with them through the use of your surveys, conversations during the social hour, and even discussions following your presentation.

ASPECT 6 - The Noise

There are *two types of noise* a speaker must contend with:

a. External Noise
b. Internal Noise

External Noise - consists of sounds, people talking, coughing, shifting patterns, poor acoustics, temperature (too warm, too cold), poor ventilation, and visual interference such as poor lighting, or an obstructed view.

Internal Noise - if a speaker is confused or unclear about what he or she wants to express, this is due to internal noise. Internal noise can also arise if the speaker does not know or does not analyze the audience.

The role of the audience and the speaker is to simultaneously communicate with each other. 'Response - ability' is the key. It is this transactional nature of speech that makes feedback, and attempts to eliminate noise, so important.

The most specific way a speaker can use to *combat noise*:

a. Use more than one channel of communication at the same time (verbal and non-verbal)
b. Use repetition and restatement.

The speaker can help combat this noise by making an extra effort to use as many channels of communications at the same time. It is important to include both verbal and non-verbal means of communication.

ASPECT 7 - The Setting

The place in which you deliver your presentation may be one that enhances or interferes with the effectiveness of your presentation. Determine ahead of time what the facilities are like <u>before</u> you speak. This way you can properly plan your delivery or make adjustments, if necessary.

There are **7 aspects** people must deal with when *preparing and delivering presentations*. An effective speaker learns to deal with all 7 aspects at the same time. Failure to pay attention to all of these aspects can result in an ineffective presentation. Failure to pay attention to too many of these can result in disaster.

1. Speaker
2. Message
3. Audience
4. Channel
5. Feedback
6. Noise
7. Setting

Keynote Address

A keynote address is designed to present the issues of primary interest to an assembly and often to arouse unity and enthusiasm.

1. **DON'T TRY TO FOOL THE AUDIENCE.** It probably won't work. Audiences are very perceptive. They know when the speaker is congruent and "walks the talk". They also know when the presenter is just giving a book report, having spent a little time in preparation to learn about the high points of the topic presented. When you are the keynoter, you have to be a fountain of knowledge.

2. **DON'T READ IT FROM YOUR TEXT**. We liked hearing stories read to us as children. But our audiences are adults. They want to experience what is in your heart and in your mind. Notes to guide you through the important points are fine, but if you are reading from a text, you may as well hire a professional actor who is trained to bring a script to life. As your audience reacts to a particular point, expand on it. Feed them what they need most.
3. **DON'T USE INSIDE STORIES**. Be sure to mention some event or some anecdote about someone that most of your audience will know nothing about. Isolate the majority of your audience. Keep them in the dark. Make them feel that they are not among the chosen few. Use their time to have a private, inside dialogue with someone.
4. **DON'T CRACK JOKES ON YOUR AUDIENCE**. Humour is a wonderful communication tool (if you are funny). Self-deprecating humor that reveals your own vulnerabilities and foibles works. Stories about people and events, other than your audience, if done in good taste, will set the tone for a positive learning environment. But if you direct the barbs of your humor directly to your audience, you set up an "us versus him/her" climate that will interfere with your message getting out. Attacking an audience, even if not meant to offend, will tend to make them defensive and distrustful of the speaker.
5. **DON'T GO OVER THE TIME LIMIT.** You have a contract with your audience. Their obligation is to be attentive. Yours is to deliver the material that was promised and to do it within the announced time frame. If you are given twenty minutes, finish in twenty minutes.

If no time frame is announced, tell the audience up front how much of their time you will take. ("We are going to be together for the next 45 minutes and during this brief time").

Tips for Conference Speaking: Stand Up, Speak Up, Shut Up

- Being invited to speak at a conference is a nice experience. Speaking at a conference is a good exercise.
- Preparing your speech focuses your mind on to the important topics you will talk about, and helps you marshal and organise your thoughts on your area of expertise
- Have a specified amount of time to speak and think how best to communicate these topics
- Nothing speeds your heart like public speaking, and most of us could do with the practice
- Engaging with other speakers helps improve your performance and it helps you see where your area fits into the wider environment
- It helps cement your reputation as an expert in a field

12 TIPS for a good conference presentation: academic and business conferences

1. Follow convention
People attend conferences to be briefed on topics which they need to know about. They have busy lives and want to leave the conference knowing something new. They want to hear an expert talk about their area of expertise, calmly, authoritatively and factually. The main rule of

public speaking – **stand up, speak up, shut up** – is the bottomline. Be interesting, be clever and be engaging, but if the organiser asks for 20 minutes on the future of the PEER PRSSURE and CYBER PRESSURE, it's because that's what he has told the delegates they will get, and it's what the delegate has paid his fee to be told. Bad speakers try to be funny or unconventional or quirky, and it usually doesn't work. Keep it simple, follow the rules and give the audience what they demand: *KISS*: *Keep It Short and Simple*.

2. Agree to the terms of reference
Usually a conference organiser will invite you to speak on a general topic and you'll agree to the points you'll cover. If you commit to covering those points, then cover them.

3. Speaking alongside a Famous Person
Conference organisers like to invite a Famous Person to give a keynote speech because it's a good hook to get people to attend their event. You might be lucky – you may be the Famous Person; if so, well done. But it's more likely that you'll be on the agenda alongside a government minister, international expert or media celebrity. Think carefully if you're scheduled to speak before or after the star – while you may be able to bathe in reflected glory, they do have a tendency to overshadow other speakers, and possibly the event as a whole. Some good speakers lose the attention of their audience when the Celebrity arrives in the middle of their speech, and all eyes turn away from the speaker and towards that person.

4. Assert yourself
You've been invited to speak at a conference because someone thinks you've something interesting to say which

the delegates should hear. You've got to explain to them why your opinion on the topic is the one they should pay attention to. Outline briefly why you know your subject matter and the audience will pay attention. Plan your speech to tell them something they didn't know or couldn't know by reading the research papers.

5. Flexibility

Do ask the organiser for a delegate list. Get a general idea of who is attending the conference and what their expectations are, and fit your presentation to that. You need to go to the audience; they won't come to you. An academic audience has very different expectations from a business audience; you should be careful to give the right speech to the right crowd. You should also fit your speech to the time of day – in general, speeches in the morning are more formal than speeches in the afternoon when the delegates have had a chance to mingle, chat and relax. If you're speaking immediately after lunch, then you've got to try twice as hard to get their attention because they'll be sleepy. If you're the last speaker of the day, then it's likely that the conference will be running late and the audience will be thinking about going home. Don't delay them or you'll be the person they blame for getting home late. These are important issues to take into account when preparing your speech.

6. Listen to previous speakers

You must at least listen to a couple of speakers before you, so you can assess the mood of the event. Each conference has its own atmosphere and a good speaker will be able to read that atmosphere and adapt their speech to fit it. Some conferences are serious and the audience will sit in silence and not ask any questions; others are more interactive and you should be able to cope with both. Good speakers who fail to read the audience give a totally inappropriate speech.

7. People can't read and listen at the same time

If you use PowerPoint and have a slide showing a complex graph, give the audience a couple of seconds to decode it before you start talking. If the audience is reading your slide, they're not listening to you. If they've been given a print-out of the presentation, it's likely they're reading it and not listening. It's also likely they've turned to the last page and are mentally counting the seconds until you reach the last slide.

Remember that people are doing this. Remember the rule – show, don't tell. If you begin your presentation by telling people you wish to discuss the four main trends in your business sector, then your audience will expect to be told what they are, and be reminded which of the four topics you're discussing at any given moment.

Ask the conference organiser if delegates will be emailed a copy of the PowerPoint or if it will be put online. If not, tell the audience you'll email it to them if they ask for it. This means they're not going to spend your presentation writing everything down for fear of missing anything. They can put down their pens, sit back and listen to you. It makes for a better presentation.

8. Keep it simple

In a 30 minute presentation (the maximum time you're likely to be given) you're not going to say everything you want, so break up your message into three or four of the most important topics. If a topic doesn't naturally fit into your overall message, miss it out and concentrate on your core issues. Look at the audience and get their feedback. Are they confused? Are they taking it in? Do they need a rest for a second? Are you boring them or confusing them? Do they need more background information? Can you skip a section? Can you miss out some of the background information and go straight to the heart of the presentation? If you're not sure what their body language is telling you, ask them. Assert and re-assert your main points throughout your speech.

9. Take time to summarise

At the end of your talk, wrap it up. Don't just finish with an abrupt "thank you" and scuttle off the stage. Take a moment to summarise your thoughts and re-assert your message.

If you run out of time ,don't skip the summary. Skip an earlier part instead.

10. Find out if you need to take questions

The conference organiser will have told you if you'll be answering questions or if there'll be a panel discussion after your speech. A good tip if you're taking questions is to repeat the question you're asked – not everyone in the audience will have heard what the question was, even if there are microphones, and the experience of repeating the question will help you gather your thoughts. Answer the question, and if you think your answer is too long, invite the questioner to make contact with you later, and discuss it over coffee or after the conference is finished.

11. Make sure to leave your contact details

If you're using PowerPoint, make sure your email address is clearly shown on your presentation. Many people will contact you and ask a question they were too nervous to ask on the day, or which only occurred to them when they got home. Even though the speech is over, you're still available on call.

12. Stand up, speak up, shut up

CHARISMA, Public Speaking and Leadership

Charisma is by definition a rare personal quality that is usually attributed to political leaders who arouse fervent popular devotion and enthusiasm. However, it is not unknown in other persons.

They are:

- personality congruency
- personality alignment
- unique depth, scope and grasp of knowledge
- deep insight
- clarity of mind and vision
- precision and direction in the decision process
- power in verbal articulation.

All these variables relate to the style of *metamentation* (thinking) and the scope command of his language.

Charisma is about a person who emanates exquisite personal charm and power. By his wish and will he can be utterly compelling and irresistible. His kindness can be overwhelming and his dark side can be utterly devastating.

How To Manage Your Behaviour

a. environment
b. Examine your behaviour; you are the book, you are the author of the book; you are the reader; write a different script; identify your goals
c. Examine assumptions that underline your behaviour; rational or irrational
d. Be aware of your feelings; to accept them, to be true to them, to learn from them, to share them
e. Psycho-cybernetics; imagine doing a thing well; increase probability of improved performance

f. Fantasy or selective memory recalling happy moments change present feeling
g. I can change my behaviour by changing my behaviour (behaviour rehearsal)

Steps to Present a Complete Self Image

- Take inventory
- Make up - dress up - go up
- Read rags to riches stories
- Be a good listener
- A series of steps
- Join the smile and compliment club
- Do something for someone else
- People around
- List your positive qualities
- Victory list of the past
- Somethings you must avoid
- Learn from successful failures
- Join an organization with worthwhile goals
- Look them in the eye
- Alter your physical appearance when possible, practical and desirable

Verbal Communication Making Presentation

- Material-should be concise, to the point and tell an interesting story (VISUAL aids)
- Voice- how you say-what you say
- Body language-body movements express your attitude and thoughts
- Appearance
- Practice is essential

3 Vs: Visual Vocal Verbal

Preparation
- Prepare the structure of your talk carefully and logically
- Objectives of the talk
- Write out presentation in rough
- Never read from a script- prepare cue cards-post cards
- Synchronise point and visual aid
- Rehearse your presentation

Making the Presentation
- Greet the audience
- INTRO- Interest, need, title, rating, objective
- Keep to the time allowed. It is better to under-run than over-run
- Don't keep on to a screen thought for too long
- Stick to the plan
- End by inviting questions

Delivery
- Speak clearly- judge the acoustics of the room
- Don't rush or talk deliberately slow. Be natural- although not conversational
- Deliberately pause at key points
- Avoid jokes
- Change pitch of voice
- Look at the audience as much as possible
- Avoid moving about too much and covering the screen
- Keep an eye on the body language of the audience

Emphasis
Work by contrast principle - emphasis changes meaning - implies contrast.

Text devices
Italics, underline, bold, size(font) punctuation, uppercase, colour

Headings
Emphasis on key points- be careful of 'ums' and 'ers'

Non-verbal Communication

Emerson "What you do speaks so loud that I cannot hear what you say"
- Facial
- Voice paralanguage
- Hand gestures
- Body movement (kinesis)
- Touch (haptics)
- Personal space

Categories and features: 4 broad categories
- Physical
- Aesthetic
- Signs
- Symbolic

Static Features	Dynamic Features
Distance	Facial expressions
Orientation	Gestures
Posture	Eye contact
Physical	Contact

Improve Nonverbal Communication: 6 Ways

1. Eye contact 2. Facial expressions 3. Gestures 4. Posture and body orientation 5. Proximity 6. Paralinguistics (tone, pitch, rhythm, timbre, loudness, inflection)

Using Cue Cards

The Three Presentation Styles

The three presentation styles:
1. **Memorize** the presentation,
2. **Write** a full script and read from it
3. **Cue cards** - Use free, conversational speech aided by some form of notes or by the using cue cards and planning cards.

   1. **Memorize:**
      (a) Time and effort
      (b) Have to concentrate - the style can become stilted.
   2. **Reading** from a fully scripted presentation invariably leads to a dull and boring monologue. It is also likely to reduce eye contact and general spontaneity, with a resultant loss of impact.

      These problems can generally only be overcome by employing a professional speechwriter to write a presentation that will be delivered by a professional actor.
   3. The use of natural conversational language assisted by **pre-prepared** cues is almost always the best style for a business presentation. It will help you to sound **normal, natural and spontaneous** and it will also create a less formal and more relaxed relationship between you and your audience.

Using Planning Cards

Placing the facts and information that you have collated into the correct position within your presentation structure is a critical process.

One of the best ways to put the facts into their optimum sequence to support the messages is to write each fact and piece of information on a separate planning card - these are typically the size of a small postcard. Then by shuffling the order around you will be able to experiment until you find a sequence which delivers the best effect.

During this process you may decide to make alterations to your original structure, changing the sequence and relationships between certain messages. Remember that it is the impact and clarity of the messages that is important, and not sticking rigidly to a structure that can be improved.

You may also find that certain facts and pieces of information are more effective in supporting an alternative message to the one which you had originally envisaged - if that is the case move the facts. Remember that the best rule of thumb to adopt when screening your research information is to stop adding facts when your point is clear and present them in order of importance.

Using Cue Cards

At this time you should have a clear picture of your presentation. You will know the overall message - that is the aim statement. You will have devised a series of key points and the messages and sub-messages- organized, in order of importance, the facts and information that you are going to use - and these will be clearly numbered. Convert your planning cards to cue cards.

These are a common presentation aid and their role is precisely as their name suggests - to cue the presenter.

This example shows how the information on a fact card might be converted to a cue card.

Fact Card

Total initial investment = Rs 425,000

Cue Card

Total initial investment = OMR 425,000

Cost Breakdown

Laptops with modems and inbuilt printer units = OMR 245,000

Quotation and lead-management software = OMR 65,000

Staff training to recognized standard = OMR 115,000

Total = OMR 425,000

Current market rate for the hardware alone is OMR 325,000 but our purchasing department has secured an offer from a leading supplier for OMR 245,000 – generating a saving of OMR 80,000. This offer remains open for 24 days from today. All hardware carries 12 month on-site replacement warranty. Written off in the accounts over 24 months but in service for 48 months.

Cue cards should hold the level of information necessary to enable you to present in a natural and seemingly spontaneous way. They are so widely used that it is usually acceptable for the presenter to hold them in one hand and refer to them openly, as required.

Only write on one side of each cue card - this avoids the distracting behavior of flipping and manipulating them and confusion as to whether or not you have addressed both sides of each spent card.

Only communicate one theme or idea on each card - this way when you have covered the point you will be confident that you can move onto the next card. Once again this avoids distracting behavior - of re-scanning cards that you have already dealt with.

Designing Effective Cue Cards

Put enough detail on each card to provide you with adequate

support and cues, but don't let it become a script. If you have too much detail you will either end up reading from the card or continually referring to it. This will be distracting and will also reduce your eye contact with the audience. Use a large font and double spacing so that the cue cards are easy to read, enabling you to take in the information at a glance. Use color coding to identify lower level information that could be dropped from the presentation in the event that the allocated time has been suddenly shortened or you find yourself overrunning. For example you might use black typeface for all the essential information and red for topics that could be omitted without compromising the integrity of the message - should you find yourself running short of time.

You might want to develop a personal shorthand system, for example a smiley face symbol could be placed at strategic points on your cue cards to remind you to make contact with the audience and smile. You might also want to annotate the cards with timing points, enabling you to keep a regular check on your progress.

Adding Timing Prompts to Cue Cards

An important feature of any presentation is the timing. The pauses can be as important as the spoken word in communicating content and meaning. It is the silences that provide the aural punctuation. When planning your delivery consider how it will sound to your audience, where you should break for the audience to take a point on board; or in order to emphasize what you have just said. Add these pauses to your cue card by writing pause at the appropriate place. A pause within a presentation should last longer than a break in normal speech - it should typically be between two and three seconds. You will be able to review the effect of this technique in the rehearsal phase and adjust it accordingly. You should now be aware of a variety of useful guidelines for writing cue cards - but the precise wording is up to you.

The only real guideline here is that you should aim to include references to the key words, phrases and examples that you will be using. Remember, the notes on your cue cards should complement the natural language style of your presentation.

Words Flagrantly Misused: Be Alert

1. The above remarks apply to all students. (Do not use remarks as an adjective: remarks above/preceding remarks)
2. Firstly I have no money, secondly I have not time. (First: There is no such word in English as 'Firstly')
3. Please consider me as your friend (regard me as/ consider me your friend)
4. Shall the windows it is fairly cold. (Fairly is used in a good sense/ rather cold)
5. Drinking tea is a English habit. (not habit/ custom)
6. He wrote shortly because he had very little paper. (Not shortly: time/ briefly: manner)
7. He has been sick for three years now. (ill not sick)
8. The magistrate issued order from his arrest. (orders)
9. Has your brother brought a new dress. (set of clothes/ suit- dress for your sister!)
10. When I entered the compartment here was no place for me. (not place but room)
11. I get a monthly allowance of hundred rupees. (a hundred…)
12. I have just taken my meals. (meal/ lunch etc)

13. May I now take your leave. (take leave of you)
14. One should always remain loyal to his company (one's country).
15. I slept rather late last night. (slept is incorrect/ went to bed)
16. I am living in Delhi. (live in)
17. He walks an if the earth belongs to him. (belongs is incorrect/ belonged)
18. Hundreds of people died by the earthquake. (died is incorrect in this context/ killed)
19. I have to give another examination this year. (Not give/take)
20. He has built a new home for himself. (house not home; Houses are built with bricks; homes are built by hearts)
21. Please write your names in ink. (in/ with)
22. I shall be back just now. (not just now/ soon or presently)
23. This book comprises of this section. (comprises does not require 'of')
24. He sat in a tree (Is correct!)

MULTUM IN PARVO: Much in Less

Build up wit and epigrams for effective communications

1. Most of our time is taken up making good, making trouble, or making excuses.
2. The person we don't like is the one who is always ME – D E E P in conversation
3. The fellow who embezzles the money always seem calm and collected.

4. If we could see ourselves as others see us, we would never want a second look.
5. Good manners consist in letting others tell you what you already know.
6. Economic lesson: Increased earnings always bring increased yearnings.
7. The reason the road to success is crowded is that it is filled with women pushing their husbands.
8. You can measure the progress of civilization by who gets more applause – the clown or the thinker.
9. Time is what passes between pay days.
10. Work is time you spend on jobs you get paid for, and leisure is time you spend on jobs you don't get paid for.
11. Destiny may shape our ends, but making ends meet is our responsibility.
12. By the time you have enough so you can sleep late in the morning, you are so old you want to get up early.
13. Life is pretty simple – you only need a comfortable bed and comfortable shoes because you are in one of the other all your life.
14. You have to be nice until you earn your first million, and after that folks will be nice to you.
15. The world is composed of Gives and Takers : the takers may eat better but it is the givers that sleep better.
16. Experience is like a comb: we generally get it when we turn bald.
17. Your head is like your pocket book because it not how it looks but what's inside that counts.
18. Nothing stretches slacks like snacks.
19. Variety is the spice of life, but it's good old monotony that brings home the groceries.

20. Early to bed and early to rise – till you make enough cash to do otherwise.
21. The trouble with people these days is that they want to reach the promised land without going through the wilderness.
22. If the knocking at the door is loud and long, it is not opportunity, its relatives.
23. There's a book that tells you where to go on your vacation. It's called a cheque book.
24. No dreams come true until you wake up and go to work.
25. No opportunity is lost, the other fellow takes it.
26. To get ahead you must use your head.
27. In the dramatically correct home the wife says. "You shall" and the husband says "I will".
28. Freedom of speech is a great thing. It even permits people to talk nonsense.
29. The most effective answer to an insult is silence.
30. The way to get into "Who's Who" is to know "What's What".
31. Some persons don't know the difference between thinking for yourself and thinking of yourself.
32. As you grow older, you grow wiser, talk less and say more.
33. Money talks and for most it is their mother tongue.
34. Nothing goes to a man's stomach as success.
35. There are five thousand languages and dialects in the world and money speaks all of them.
36. There are great many books now on how to live longer, but none on why.
37. If you rest your chin on your hand when you think, it will help you to keep your mouth closed.

38. To reach a great height a person needs to have depth.
39. Vacation is the period you spend two weeks in an old shack without conveniences so you can go back to your home with its comforts and complain.
40. On way to get rid of weight is to leave it on the plate.

Rhetoric of the Classicals: The Basis of Communication

Art of Persuasion

Distinction between content and form: *what* is said and *how* we say it.

Logos Lexis

Tripartite distinction between appeals:

- Logos, or appeal to reason;
- Pathos, or appeal to emotion; and
- Ethos, or the appeal to character.

3 way of rhetoric:

- Kairos, or the occasions for speech-contexts for a speech
- Audience, or who will hear or read it
- Decorum , or fitting words and subject together

Rhetorical Devices

Expletives-synonymous with swear words

In brief, you should be more careful.
The result was to be expected, of course.

Similes, Analogies and Metaphors

Simile – A simile involves comparing two things-involves words such as "like', "as" or "does'.

Her smile was like sunshine.
He was as silent as a church mouse

Analogy

Analogies – also invites a comparison used to explain a difficult concept

He did in the figure of a lamb the feats of a lion.

Metaphor

The Sultan is a lion

Metonymy – involves a metaphor where is comparison is with something associated but not with identical to the target of discussion:

- The crown is powerful
- The state cares little for my concerns.

Personification – we ascribe human characteristics to objects or situations

- Truth is no respecter of hopes.
- Fortune smiled on him.

Hyperbole

Sometimes we overstate things for rhetorical effect:

- There were millions of people at the bus stop today.
- It took me for ever to finish the essay.

Understatement – is something satirists use-believe the person is in error

- Your analysis is far too simplistic

Litotes – is an understatement formed by the denial of an opposite.

Performances like that from that group are not uncommon.

Questions

- **Hypophora** – posing a question before nominating one to answer.
- **Rhetorical (or erotesis)** – a question asked but deliberately does not require an answer :What kind of person would bet against the sun rising tomorrow, though?
- **Procatalepsis** – when questions are asked and answered by the writer or speaker, usually by anticipating objections: It is often thought that the only way to address poverty is via governmental initiatives. However, I would advocate a greater role for…

Asyndetons and Polysyndetons

The Oman soccer team has power, grace, speed and strength. (no 'and' between speed and strength' – seems the list could have gone on.

I wasted my afternoon reading, writing, thinking, dreaming.

These are examples of *asyndetons* when conjunctions are left out to achieve this sense of diversity, or even add emphasis by what seems like an afterthought;

- Bond was a wizard, a master.
- Bond was a wizard and a master.

Apostrophe

This is a direct address to the dead, to the absent, or to a personified object or idea. This figure is a special form of personification..

Hyerbole

A statement is made emphatic by overstatement.

e.g.. Here's the smell of blood still; all the perfumes of Arabia will not sweeten this little hand.

Euphemism
This consists in the description of a disagreeable thing by an agreeable name.

He has fallen asleep. (dead)
You are telling me a fairy tale (i.e. a lie)

Antithesis – a striking opposition or contrast of words or sentiments is made in the same sentence. It is employed to secure emphasis.

Man proposes, God deposes.

Oxymoron – Oxymoron is a special form of antithesis, whereby two contradictory qualities are predicted at once of the same thing.

His honour rooted in dishonour stood.

Figure of Speech

A *figure of speech* or a *trope* (the latter word has a more specific use) is a non-ordinary use of language employed to create an emphasis, amplify a meaning, draw a comparison or contrast, or to make a rhetorical point. The figure may be achieved by employing-

- repetition of words or sounds in a specific pattern,
- making an interjection,
- stating or implying a comparison,
- using synonyms, or using a specific pattern of argument.

More on Rhetoric

Ad Hominem
Literally this means "towards the man". Refers to a negative or scurrilous remark (often name calling) attacking the

person of one's opponent rather than arguing the substance of the matter at hand.

Secondary Category: negative

e.g. You believe that (voted for.. etc.) You're an idiot, a fool.

Amplification

This means the expansion upon an idea in greater detail or depth.

e.g. So much for the definition. Now let me explain in detail.

Anabasis *or Gradual Ascent*

This is an increase of emphasis on some meaning in successive sentences.

e.g. Blessed is the man that walketh not in the counsel of the ungodly, nor standeth in the way of sinners, nor sitteth in the seat of the scornful. (Psalm 1:1)

Anastrophe

This is an inversion of the natural order of words.

e.g. Long hours worked the men. instead of The men worked long hours.

Aphorism

This is a concise statement or popular saying that expresses a principle or truth in a terse manner. Usually shorter than a proverb, and may have an element of the trite.

e.g. People who live in glass houses shouldn't throw stones.

Aporia

Here the speaker expresses doubt about his or her position or asks rhetorically how to proceed.

e.g. How shall I put this?

Aposiopesis

This is a form of ellipsis, in which the speaker breaks off suddenly in the middle of speaking, giving the impression of being unwilling or unable to continue, perhaps portraying being overcome with emotion.

e.g. This outrage is beyond all...

Axiom

This is a self-evident truth, generally accepted idea, or undefined term upon which other knowledge rests, or is built up.

Secondary Category: logic

e.g. Two points determine a line.

Belittling

This is a lessening of one thing, person, or idea in order to magnify a competing one.

e.g. His clothes were so yesterday.

Catabasis *or Gradual Descent*

This means an decrease of emphasis on some meaning in successive sentences.

e.g. Who, being in the form of God, thought it not robbery to be equal with God: But made himself of no reputation, and took upon him the form of a servant, and was made in the likeness of men: And being found in fashion as a man, he humbled himself, and became obedient unto death, even the death of the cross. (Philippians 2:6-8)

Notes: May be used to emphasize humiliation, sorrow. The opposite of anabasis.

Ellipsis

Words omitted from a sentence or phrase that would be necessary to complete the formal grammar (syntax) but are not needed for the meaning (semantics).

e.g. 1, 2, 3, ... 10

Notes: Indicated in written material with three dots.

Enigma

A dark or obscure saying or puzzling statement or an obscure mystery not yet explained. It may be expressed of persons and events as well as of things.

Secondary Category: riddle

e.g. The riddle of the sphinx: What walks first on four legs, then on two, and later on three?

Notes: Once the riddle has been solved, it is, of course, no longer an enigma."

Enthymeme

A syllogism with part of the argument assumed rather than stated.

e.g. Socrates is mortal because he is human. (The major premise is implicit, not stated.)

Erotesis *or Rhetorical question(s)*

The asking of (perhaps multiple) questions without awaiting an answer.

Secondary Category: answer

e.g. If you prick us, do we not bleed? —Shakespeare's Merchant of Venice

Notes: The meaning must be gleaned by putting the question into a statement. The question always has an obvious answer.

Hyperbaton *or Transposition*

The deliberate or accidental placing of a word out of its usual order in a sentence or dramatic departure from standard syntax (word order) for poetic effect.

Secondary Category: Grammar

e.g. Quoth the Raven, "Nevermore." (E. A. Poe)

Notes: Often used with an adjective or pronoun, or by reversing noun and verb.

Litotes

A deliberate usage of understatement to enhance the quality of what was said. One might emphasize the magnitude of a statement by denying its opposite.

e.g. 1. One nuclear bomb could spoil your whole day. 2. The pastor was not ignorant of doctrine. 3. The winning book wasn't bad.

Meiosis *or Diminution*

Intentionally understating or belittling something or implying it is less in significance or size, than it really is.

e.g. 1. It's only a scratch. 2. He was a citizen of no mean city (Acts 21:39)

Metonymy *or Denominatio*

The the use of a single characteristic to identify a more complex entity.

Secondary Category: rhetoric

e.g.:

1. "In an early morning press conference, Number 10 Downing Street today said…"
2. "The pen is mightier than the sword.

Oxymoron

An expression or phrase (usually two words) that appears to be or is alleged to be self-contradictory.

e.g. 1. Hysterical rationalism 2. Military intelligence

Paraprosdokian

An ending to a sentence or phrase that is unexpected given the prior construction. It can be used for levity or for dramatic effect.

e.g. It was a beautiful day in March when the building fell on me.

Paroemia *or Proverb*
A succinct or pithy expression of what is commonly observed and believed to be true.

e.g. 1. The fear of the LORD is the beginning of knowledge, but fools despise wisdom and discipline. (Proverbs 1:7) 2. Of making many books there is no end, and much study wearies the body. (Ecclesiates 12:12)

Periphrasis *or Circumlocution*
Defining or explaining a single word or concept with many words, can also have the sense of talking around the subject and avoiding coming to the point.

e.g. The woman whom I married thirty years ago and to whom I am still happily married. (instead of "my wife")

Notes: Any definition of a word (which is generally in terms of several other words) is periphrastic. Circumlocution is also at times evasive, an attempt to avoid answering a question."

Praeteritio *or Paralipsis*
Emphasis is achieved by stating that the speaker is passing something by.

e.g. 1. Not to mention... 2. I won't dignify that with a response. 3. Pay no attention to that fellow over there.

Procatalepsis
Raising an objection and immediately answering it; strengthening an argument by dealing with possible objections before the audience can raise counter arguments.

e.g. You may think programming difficult to understand, but if you bear with me I will show you how to break the discipline into steps.

Proslepsis
An extreme form of paralipsis

e.g. I will not mention my opponents numerous criminal convictions. It would be unseemly to bring them up again.

Syllogism

A three part logical argument consisting of a major premise or general rule followed by a minor premise or instance of the precondition in the rule, and then a conclusion based on applying the major premise to its instance.

e.g. Rule or major premise: All humans are mortal. Minor premise: Socrates is human. Conclusion: Socrates is mortal.

Tapeinosis *or Demeaning*

An attempt to lessen the importance of a thing, person or idea. Also called a put-down, though with more negative, perhaps scornful overtones.

e.g. He was a pimple on the body of history.

Notes: Differs from meiosis in that the outcome is a person's humiliation.

Tsmeis

A word, phrase, or portion thereof is inserted into another word.

e.g. whatsoever

Repetition

Anadiplosis *or Like Endings and Beginnings*

A "doubling back" or repetition of the same word or words from the end of one sentence or clause at the beginning of another.

e.g. Men in great place are thrice servants: servants of the sovereign or state; servants of fame; and servants of business. — Francis Bacon

Anaphora *or Like-Beginnings*
The repetition of the same word or phrase at the beginning of successive clauses or sentences.

e.g. We shall fight on the beaches, we shall fight on the landing grounds, we shall fight in the fields and in the streets, we shall fight in the hills. (Winston Churchill)

Antanaclasis
A repetition of the same word in the same sentence or in very close proximity but with two different meanings.

e.g. They cast lots to see which of the two lots they would be buying.

Assonance
The repetition of vowel sounds within a short passage.

e.g. Moses supposes his toeses are roses.

Notes: Generally used in poetry, not prose."

Chiasmus
From the Greek letter chi, shaped like the Latin X, and meaning a crossing. Two entities are related to one another in a "crossing" structure.

e.g. 1. I love you as you love me. 2. "Ask not what your country can do for you — ask what you can do for your country." (John F. Kennedy)

Climax *or Gradation*
Continuous anadiplosis - repetition of endings and beginnings of a particular sentence or clause.

Secondary Category: logic

e.g. II Peter 1:5

Notes: Each of the repeated concepts is important in the sequence of argument.

Double (Multiple) Negation
Use of two or more negatives in close proximity. Formal'y,

this would imply a positive, but the usual effect is to emphasize the negative.

e.g. He don't got no dough.

Notes: Can be the combination of a negative verb with a negative conjunction.

Epanadiplosis *or Encircling*
Repetition of the same word or words at the beginning and end of a sentence or sentence group.

e.g. Rejoice in the Lord always, and again I say, Rejoice. Philippians 4:4

Notes: Consider the encircled sentences as a unit of thought.

Epanados *or Inversion*
Repetition of different words in a sentence in an inverse order but with a similar meaning.

e.g. Make the heart of this people fat, and make their ears heavy, and shut their eyes; lest they see with their eyes, and hear with their ears, and understand with their heart, and convert, and be healed. (Isaiah 6:10)

Epanalepsis *or Resumption*
Repetition of a word, phrase, or idea following any kind of parenthesis in order to return to the original thought..

e.g. See 1Cor.10:29; Phil.1:24 for instances of this.

Notes: Marks return to a previous subject, possibly following a paranthetical remark."

Epibole
Repetition of the same phrase at irregular intervals.

e.g. c.f. Psalm 29: 3-9

Notes: Differs from anaphora and repetition by being a phrase not just one word.

Epistrophe *or Like Endings*
Repetition of the same word or words at the end of successive clauses or sentences.

e.g. I yearn more to learn more that I may earn more.

Epizeuxis *or Duplication*
Repetition of the same word in immediate succession.

e.g. Isaiah 26:3

Notes: The effect is to emphasize or establish the word duplicated.

Homeopropheron *or Alliteration*
Repetition of the same letter or syllable at the commencement of two or more successive words.

e.g. Peter Piper picked a peck of pickled peppers

Notes: Tongue twisters are among the more common alliterations.

Paradiastole *or Neither-Nor*
Repetition of the disjunctive pair "neither" and "nor".

Secondary Category: disjunctives

e.g. For I am convinced that neither death nor life, neither angels nor demons, neither the present nor the future, nor any powers, neither height nor depth, nor anything else in all creation, will be able to separate us from the love of God. (Romans 8:38-39)

Polyptoton *or Many Inflections*
Repetition of the same noun in different inflections or the same verb in different conjugations.

e.g. ...had, having, and in quest to have, extreme... — Shakespeare, Sonnet 129

Notes: This may be a verb with a related noun/adjective. Common in Semitic languages.

Rhyme
Repetition of words similar in ending sound but not necessarily in sense or origin.

e.g. Little baby fast asleep, wishing you don't make a peep. Big brown eyes smile so sweet. Little baby fast asleep.

Synonymia
The use of several synonyms in succession to add emotional force or clarity.

e.g. She was lovely, beautiful, gorgeous, a paragon of femininity.

Parenthesis

Anaeresis *or Detraction*
A negative parenthetic addition that is complete in itself.

Secondary Category: negative

e.g. When I was last in Paris—but you wouldn't know what Paris is like, now would you dear—I stopped at the most divine restaurant.

Apostrophe
A form of aside directed in an abstract direction.

e.g. 1. Ah, sword of the Lord! How long till you are quiet? (JeremiahJeremiah. 47:6). 2. O Death, where is thy sting? (1 Corinthians 15:55) 3. O Christmas tree, O Christmas tree...

Aside
Turning from the immediate hearers or from the subject at hand to address an absent or imaginary person or thing.

e.g. See Iago in Shakespeare's Othello addressing the audience and informing them of his plans.

Cataploce *or Exclamation*
An emphatic parenthetic addition that is complete in itself.

e.g. God forbid!

Notes: Exclamation differs from interjection in that it usually involves an emotional response.

Epitrechon *or Remark (Running Along)*
A parenthetic addition that is not complete in itself, but requires the context to be understood.

Secondary Category: explanation

e.g. And he said unto Abram, Know of a surety that thy seed shall be a stranger in a land that is not theirs, and shall serve them; and they shall afflict them four hundred years. (Genesis 15:13)

Hypotimesis *or Under-Estimating*
A minimizing parenthetic addition complete in itself. Usually used to express an apology for what might otherwise be taken amiss.

e.g. To my shame I admit that we were too weak for that! What anyone else dares to boast about—I am speaking as a fool— I also dare to boast about. (2 Corinthians 11:21)

Interjection
A parenthetic addition that may not share the surrounding grammatical structure, but is complete in itself.

e.g. Here they come now. Look out! The black is about to overtake for the lead.

Parembole *or Digression*
A complete parenthetic addition that bears little if any overt relationship with the surrounding material.

e.g. And David took the head of the Philistine, and brought it to Jerusalem; but he put his armour in his tent. (1 Samuel 17:54).

Parenthesis *or Interpositio*

An addition complete in itself, understandable only in its context, but without necessarily any grammatical connection to the surrounding text. The parenthesis may be an illustration of the context or a near-digression into a tangential topic.

e.g. So when you see standing in the holy place 'the abomination that causes desolation', spoken of through the prophet Daniel—let the reader understand—then let those who are in Judea flee to the mountains. (Matthew 24:15-16)

Notes: A parenthesis differs from a digression in that it provides an explanation of the material in the surrounding context. That is, the main subject has not been changed. The parenthesis may be an illustration."

Meaning

Anthimeria

e.g. The knight was unhorsed. The use of a word of one class as though it were a member of another, typically the use of a noun as a verb.

Antithesis

A seeming contradiction of ideas, words, clauses, or sentences creating a parallelism that serves to emphasize opposition of ideas.

e.g. The king proposes, parliament disposes.

Antonomasia *or Name Change*

Change of proper name for a common or other name or vice versa.

Secondary Category: names

e.g. Have you seen old sideburns lately?

Notes: This is often a descriptive nickname. The description takes place of the literal name.

Auxesis
Magnifying the importance of something by giving it another name. It can be the opposite of Meiosis.

e.g. Two dollars for that piece of junk? That's highway robbery!

Catachresis *or Incongruity*
Two items compared or one standing for the other when the ideas they represent are radically different or perhaps contradictory, paradoxical or contradictory logic, or an illogical mixed metaphor.

e.g. To take arms against a sea of troubles. Ð William Shakespeare

Eiderism
Pointing out that two words that normally mean the opposite can mean the same thing or be part of the same meaning, when used in the right context.

e.g. "Drink it up" and "Drink it down" illustrate that "up" and "down" can in a sense mean the same thing, or manner.

Eironeia *or Irony*
The expression of thought in a form that emphasizes or conveys the opposite meaning to the words used. A tone of voice may be necessary to convey irony if the words are not intended to be taken at face value.

e.g. 1. ...you are the people and wisdom will die with you (Job 12:1). 2. For Brutus is an honourable man; So are they all, honorable men. —Shakespeare, Julius Caesar

Notes: The surface meaning and the underlying meaning are not the same. Irony may be biting or sarcastic, and often has negative or pejorative overtones."

Enallage
One part of speech is used for another, or one grammatical form is substituted for another, such as present for past or singular for plural.

e.g. Think different.

Euphemism
A word or phrase commonly used in place of terms which are disagreeable or offensive.

e.g. My uncle passed away last fall.

Hendiadys *or Two for One*
Two words with similar or identical meanings are used where one would be sufficient.

e.g. The Latin expression "cum amicitia atque pace", literally "with peace and friendship" might be rendered in English as "with friendly peace", changing one of the redundant nouns into an adjective.

Notes: The combination of concepts that more often are described with a different word combining the two ideas.

Hendiatris *or Three for One*
Three words used but one thing meant.

e.g. ...how can we know the way? Jesus said to him, I am the way, the truth, and the life: no man comes to the Father, but by me. (John 14: 5-6)

Notes: In this example, the question concerned the way, but it is answered threefold."

Heterosis *or Exchange*
Exchange of one accidence or part of speech for another.

e.g. 1. In many languages. Collectives such as mankind which are both male and female are deemed for grammatical purposes to be male. 2. She run all the way to the store.

Notes: Frequently used with the gender of nouns or with verb tenses.

Homographs
Words that are identical in spelling but different in origin and meaning
   e.g. invalid, row, sewer, wound

Homonyms
Words that are identical with each other in pronunciation and spelling, but differing in origin and meaning.
   e.g. age, reflect, arithmetic, high, report, rest

Homophones
Words that are identical with each other in pronunciation, but differing in origin, spelling, and meaning.
   e.g. 1. ant, aunt 2. leased, least 3. oh, owe

Hypallage *or Interchange*
The normal usage of two words is swapped to make a connection in meaning.
   e.g. Open the day, and see if it be the window.—The Garden of Eloquence by Willard Espy

Hyperbole
An intentional and often considerable exaggeration or extravagant statement to make a much lesser point. The statement is not meant to be taken literally.
   e.g. 1. If your right eye causes you to sin, pluck it out and throw it away... (Matt. 5:29). 2. I could eat an ox. 3. If I've told you once I've told you a thousand times. Don't exaggerate.
   Notes: The opposite is understatement.

Idiom
A use of words and phrases peculiar to a particular language, culture, or time period.
   Secondary Category: unusual usage

e.g. 1. The spirit is willing but the flesh is weak. 2. I've got a frog in my throat. (In French it would be a cat.)

Notes: Because an idiom is particular to language or culture it may make no sense at all if translated literally.

Innuendo *or Double entendre*
An indirect and subtle implication in an expression in speech or writing, whereby a sentence has a double meaning.

e.g. When offered $40 per day strike pay to go out on an illegal strike, I said "You can keep your forty pieces of silver".

Merismos *or Distribution*
An enumeration or elaboration of the parts of some whole that has previously been mentioned.

e.g. morning and evening" means the whole day

Metalepsis *or Double Metonymy*
Two metonymies contained in one another but with only one explicitly expressed.

e.g. I've got a black thumb.

Notes: There are at least two steps to discover the meaning. In the example, the idea of a green thumb is associated with having the ability to make things grow, but black is associated with death, so in two stages we arrive at a would-be gardener whose efforts are usually fatal to the plants."

Metonymy *or Denominatio*
The the use of a single characteristic to identify a more complex entity.

Secondary Category: rhetoric

e.g. 1. "In an early morning press conference, Number 10 Downing Street today saidÉ" 2. "The pen is mightier than the sword.

Onomatopoeia
A word or group of words has a sound similar to the thing being described.
   e.g. buzz, quack, miaow, squeak, bang

Paradox
A statement that seems to lead to an illogical contradiction, or to a situation that contradicts common intuition. The statement contains the seeds of its own negation or contradiction, though this may not be apparent on the surface.
   Secondary Category: logic
   e.g. 1. The barber shaves all the men who don't shave themselves, and no-one else. 2. Let A be the set of all sets that do not contain themselves.

Pleonasm
The use of more words than necessary.
   e.g. 1. I know that he is here. 2. We hired him to head up the program.

Spoonerism
A transposition of the beginning and endings of words in a sentence that has strange or humorous effects. After Reverend Spooner (1844 - 1930)
   e.g. Spooner allegedly once praised Her Majesty with a toast to our queer old dean. Was this extremely mad banners on his part?

Syllepsis
One word modifies two or more other words simultaneously but must be understood differently with respect to each modified word. This creates a possibly humorous semantic incongruity.
   e.g. He emptied the whiskey bottle and his mind.

Synathroesmus *or Enumeration*
An enumeration or elaboration of the parts or qualities of a whole that has not necessarily been mentioned, but is at least implied.

e.g. He's a proud, haughty, consequential, turned-up-nosed peacock.Ê- Charles Dickens in Nicholas Nickleby

Synecdoche
A type of metonymy in which a part is exchanged for the whole, an individual for an entire class or people, OR vice-versa (whole for part).

Secondary Category: exchange

e.g. 1. And we were in all 276 souls. (Acts 27:37) 2. Joe ranched nearly five hundred head. 3. All hands on deck

Synonym
Refers to words that are usually different in sound and origin but are similar in meaning

e.g. Big, large, grand, tall, enormous, extended, humungous are all synonyms

Trope
The use of a word in other than its literal or normal form.

e.g. The four kinds of trope are: metonymy, irony, metaphor, and synecdoche.

Comparison

Allegory
A story, narrative, or fable in which a moral principle or truth is presented by means of fictional characters and events which stand symbolically for real persons or events.

e.g. Psalm 80:8 ff portrays God planting and tending Israel as a vineyard. Bunyan's Pilgrim's Progress is an extended allegory of the Christian life. Edmund Spenser's

The Faerie Queene is a well-known allegorical poem. Animal Farm is another example in prose.

Allusion
An indirect reference to a person, place or event made by mentioning or quoting a characteristic or aspect of the thing alluded to. Often A reference in one literary work to a character or theme found in another literary work.

e.g. He had my head on a platter. (allusion to John the Baptist)

Anthropomorphism *or Condescension*
1. A person of higher rank reaches down to one of lower rank to communicate or establish a relationship. 2. The ascribing of human attributes to God.

e.g. God's eye was upon me, his hand was with me, his arm guided me.

Hypocatastasis *or Implication*
A comparison that is suggested or hinted at by context without being explicitly stated.

e.g. But be on your guard against the yeast of the Pharisees and Sadducees. (Matthew 6:11)

Notes: This is similar to a metaphor but without any use of the verb to be. In the example, it is doctrine that is at issue. The comparison is made by a substitution, which calls more attention to the implied comparison."

Metaphor
A comparison by making a statement that one thing is another.

e.g. Benjamin is a ravenous wolf... (Gen. 49:27).

Notes: The comparison is implied by the statement of equality, not explicitly stated as in a simile."

Parable
A story told to illustrate a religious, moral or philosophical idea.

Secondary Category: illustration

e.g. The Biblical parable of the Prodigal son or of the Good Samaritan

Notes: Can be an extended simile. There may be multiple points of comparison. Parable is a broader term in Semitic thinking than in Greek.

Paronomasia *or Pun*
A play on words that rearranges the meanings of words with similar sounds, usually for humorous effect.

e.g. 1. O pun the door! 2. A door is not a door if it is ajar. 3. Very punny. 4. You are Peter and on this rock I will build my church. (Matt 16:18) 4. That was a foul tasting turkey.

Prosopopoeia *or Personification*
Things or ideas are loaned the qualities or attributes of persons.

Secondary Category: illustration

e.g. 1. The sea looked and fled...(Ps. 114:3, 4). 2. My old tin lizzy whined and limped up the hill, complaining against my foot on the accelerator.

Simile
An overt or formal declaration that one thing is "like" or "as" another, usually using one of those two words.

e.g. Even so, husbands should love their own wives as their own bodies... (Eph. 5:28).

Syncrisis
Repeated similes in close proximity.

Secondary Category: simile

e.g. We rejoice in victory; they despair in defeat.

Epigrams and Witticisms

- An optimistic gardener is a person who believes that what goes down must come up.
- Most of our time is taken up making good, making trouble, or making excuses.
- It's not too hard to live with your own faults, but it's hard to put up with the faults of others.
- The person we don't like is the one who is always me-deep in conversation.
- A luxury is something you don't need but feel you can't do without.
- Nowadays no farmer counts his chickens till he crosses the road.
- The fellow who embezzles the money always seems calm and collected.
- If we could see ourselves as others see us, we would never want a second look.
- Good manners consist in letting others tell you what you already know.
- There has been only one indispensable man, and that was Adam.
- The family that isn't in debt today is underprivileged.
- Travel flattens the purse, broadens the mind, and lengthens the conversation.
- To train children at home, it is necessary for both parents and children to spend sometime there.
- Some persons are the kind of friends who stand by you – with their arms folded.
- The bridegroom fainted on the way to his wedding. Wait till he gets the first month's bills.
- A nation needs a foreign policy that is not patterned after its weather policy.

- One thing you learn from experience is that you can't make money without working.
- A pessimist is an optimist who voted for a politician he thought would reduce government spending.
- By the time you get enough experience to be able to watch your step, you may not be going anywhere.
- You can lose your shirt by putting too much on your cuff.
- More people would try to do right if they thought it was wrong.
- A brilliant conversationalist is a person who uses meaningless words to say a great deal about nothing.
- If you don't know what to be thankful for, be thankful for all the trouble you haven't had.
- When an apple a day costs more than keeping a doctor away, brother, that's inflation!
- No one has inside information as good as the doctor's.
- The best thing parents can spend on children is time – not money.
- Nothing is further than the distance between advice and help.
- Most ideas are not unusual, but the experience of having ideas is unusual.
- If we didn't have confidence in each other, we could not live beyond our incomes.
- Success in life generally expands the waistband or hatband.
- Economics lesson: increased earnings always bring increased yearnings.
- When someone says, "I do not wish to appear critical", it means he is going to let you have it.
- Solomon said, "There is no new thing under the sun", but he didn't say it over colour television.

- The world would be pretty bad if the teenagers didn't have any more sense than we sometimes think they have.
- Some people not only believe everything they hear but repeat it.
- Nothing is more difficult than trying to find something wrong with yourself.
- The reason the road to success is crowded is that it is filled with women pushing their husbands.
- When everyone approves of what you are doing, you ought to ask yourself what's wrong.
- You can measure the progress of civilization by who gets more applause – the clown or the thinker.
- Time is what passes between paydays.
- On a bus there is no such thing as the rising generation.
- It isn't easy to get an idea into a head filled with prejudices.
- A cat doesn't have nine lives, but catty remarks do.
- Work is time you spend on jobs you get paid for, and leisure is time you spend on jobs you don't get paid for.
- It isn't easy for a husband to get back some of his take home pay after he takes home.
- The fellow who watches the clock need not worry about his future because he probably hasn't any.
- We all want to live for a long time, but no one wants to get old.
- Destiny may shape our ends, but makings ends meet is our responsibility.
- He who laughs last must have time to waste.
- Years make all of us old and very few of us wise.
- Your best friends are generally those who don't meet very often.

- One thing comes to the man who waits, and that's whiskers.
- Most of us stand adversity, but prosperity is another matter.
- By the time you save enough so you can sleep late in the morning, you are so old you want to get up early.
- Life is pretty simple – you only need a comfortable bed and comfortable shoes because you are in one or the other all your life.
- A reckless driver may get to places a little sooner – even the cemetery.
- You have to be nice until you earn you first million, and after that folks will be nice to you.
- If ignorance is blessed, we should have a great many more happy people.
- When a person starts bragging about what he has done, he is getting old.
- You can go crazy in the world today without anyone noticing it.
- Sometimes a man tries to make a name for him-self by signing it to someone else's check.
- Some day some smart government is going to get the idea of spending only what it can pay for.
- Misfortune is a point of view. Your headache feels well to an aspirin salesman.
- It's strange that the fellow who always wants the most has the least with which to buy it.
- Modern youngsters are precocious. They don't read, but name any CD and they can tell you, what's on the other side.
- A man's hair is either parted or departed.
- The hardest rupee to earn is the one you have already spent.

- The person who leaves becomes the life of the party.
- There is no special relation between what you want and what you need and this makes selling interesting.
- You can sleep on a matter before you decide, unless you have a competitor who doesn't need the sleep.
- We like the person who tells us all the nice things about ourselves that we always knew.
- Women keep a secret well, but sometimes it takes quite a few of them to do it.
- It's always easier to have a courageous conviction after you know what the boss thinks.
- It only takes one to start a quarrel but it takes two to keep it up.
- Nothing shocks most of us so much as finding that we may be wrong.
- Many persons would like to do something for a living that doesn't involve work.
- Experience is what helps you recognize the same mistake as you keep on making it.
- Experience is like a comb: we generally get it when we turn bald!
- After an election speech, the audience draws its own confusions.
- Distance lends enchantment to the view, but not when you have a flat tyre.
- By piling on the dirt when you gossip, you can make a mountain out of a molehill.
- Your head is like your pocket book because it's not how it looks but what's inside that counts.
- People who seldom speak aren't the only ones who don't say much.
- It's what the guests say after they say goodnight that counts.

- Half the world doesn't know how many installments the other half is behind.
- Just because you blow your top doesn't mean you have a dynamic personality.
- Nothing is more trying than to have the neighbours buy things you can't afford.
- There are two kinds of conceited persons: those who admit it and those who don't.
- Bumper sticker to end all bumper stickers: "DON'T YOU FEEL STUPID READING THIS BUMPER STICKER THAT HAS NO MESSAGE?"
- There is no feel like an old feel. You just can't beat experience.
- Always borrow money from a pessimist – he never expects to be paid back.
- The only thing that gives you more for your money today than it did a year ago is a weighing machine.
- The world is composed of givers and takers, the takers may eat better but the givers sleep better.
- Nothing stretches slacks like snacks.
- Courage is also what it takes to stand up and speak; courage is needed more for what it takes to sit down and listen.
- What the condition a man is in can best be judged from what he takes two at a time – stairs or pills.
- The best substitute for experience is being seventeen years old.
- A reckless driver is one who passes you on the road, despite anything you can do.
- A good listener is one who can give you his full attention without hearing a word you say.
- The beginning of wisdom is silence. The second step is listening.

- Variety may be the spice of life, but it's good old monotony that brings home the groceries.
- Early to bed and early to rise – till you make enough cash to do otherwise.
- The trouble with having a doctor who doesn't make house calls is you have to be in pretty good health to find out how sick you are.
- The trouble with people these days is that they want to reach the promised land without going through the wilderness.
- When you begin to notice how much fun the young folks have you are getting old.
- Nowadays apples are so expensive you might as well have a doctor.
- If you look like your passport photo, you aren't well enough to travel.
- If the knocking at the door is loud and long, it isn't opportunity, its relatives.
- When life knocks you to your knees, you're in a position to pray.
- There's a book that tells you where to go on your vacation. It's called a chequebook.
- There's one advantage to the music the younger generation goes for today: nobody can whistle it.
- Train up a child in the way he should go, and when he gets older he will tell you how wrong you were.
- People are peculiar – they want the front of the bus, the back of the church and the middle of the road.
- Don't be afraid of asking a dumb question: that's better than making a dumb mistake.
- A good wife laughs at her husband's jokes, not because they are clever, but because she is.
- A good test of your power of concentration is your

ability to do your child's homework while he is watching television.
- What is so simple even a small child can manipulate it? A grandparent.
- When you sing your own praises, it's generally a solo.
- It's surprising how long you remember a kind deed if you did it.
- Most wallets wouldn't be so fat today if you took out the credit cards.
- If you want more leisure, get to your appointments on time.
- You can stand still and watch the world go by – and it certainly will.
- You get on best when you don't try to tell people where to get off.
- No dream comes true until you wake up and go to work.
- By the time you get the installments paid, the luxury you bought is a necessity.
- You may out bluff another driver, but the real question is whether you will outlive him.
- You are young only once and that excuse won't last forever.
- The world isn't getting smaller. The missiles just go farther.
- When business is slow. It's a good idea to give it a push.
- One thing about getting old is that you can sing in the bathroom while brushing your teeth.
- If people said what they thought, our conversation would be very brief.
- A person who lives within his income is sometimes crowded for space.

- No opportunity is lost the other fellow takes it.
- It isn't as hard to get the things you want, as it is to keep from getting the things you don't want.
- You can't make troubles for others without a little of it rubbing of on you.
- The way to end an argument is to keep your mouth shut.
- Three square meals every day and you will soon be round.
- Unfortunately, laziness is never fatal.
- A swelled head always picks out an empty one to expand.
- A hammer may miss its mark, but a compliment never.
- Doing nothing gets pretty tiresome because you can't stop and rest.
- You may be a fine upstanding citizen, but it makes no difference on a slippery sidewalk.
- Some persons are poor listeners because it interferes with what they want to say.
- Getting rattled may be a sing that there is a screw loose somewhere.
- To get ahead you have to use your head.
- A girl loves a boy's voice when it has a ring in it.
- A loose nut can cause an auto accident, but so can a tight nut.
- Today no one is so poor that he has to live within his income.
- Don't worry too much about people think, because they seldom do.
- The brain seldom wears out, probably because it seldom overworked.
- The fellow who saves the church is loosing ground is probably the same one who says the sun is loosing heat.

- It's easier for a woman to get her face lifted than it is for her husband to lift his when the bill comes in.
- Some persons are born good and others have to make good.
- In the dramatically correct home the wife says, "you shall" and the husband says, "I will".
- A successful businessman keeps his head up and his overhead down.
- None but the brave can affords the fair.
- We like the fellow who says he is going to make a long story short and does.
- We suppose a fat man dressed up is an illustration of spic and span.
- Where do bad boys and girls go, just about everywhere?
- When both a speaker and an audience are confused, the speech is profound.
- Why does a woman apologize when friends drop in unexpectedly and find the house looking like it usually does?
- Most women have a skin they love to retouch.
- June is the month when the bride who has never had a broom in her hands sweeps up the aisle.
- Money has wings and most of us see the tail feathers.
- Men are either born with consciences or marry them.
- A saver grows rich by seeming poor. A spender grows poor by seeming rich.
- The person who is ignorant can speak freely.
- Fortunately, there are always enough crises in the world to help us keep our minds off our personal problems.
- One way to find out what a woman really thinks of you is to marry her.

- Indigestion happens when there has been too much of a good thing.
- The reason a man dies suddenly in harness is that he has been working like a horse.
- Freedom of speech is a great thing. It even permits some people to talk nonsense.
- The fellow who laughs at his trouble never runs out of things at which to laugh.
- Conversation without a touch of scandal gets very dull for most people.
- Ignorance combined with silence is sometimes mistaken for wisdom.
- The person who thinks before he speaks is silent most of the time.
- When a man doesn't believe today that he believed yesterday, how could he be so confident today knowing that tomorrow is coming?
- A fisherman is the only person who tells a lie with his arms stretched out.
- Every young man knows when the right girl comes along because she tells him.
- The most effective answer to an insult is silence.
- You can't mind your own business if you haven't any mind and any business.
- There is no use in worrying about your old troubles when you know new ones will be coming along.
- It's surprising how soon a child learns how to train its parents.
- When some women promise to be on time, it carries a lot of wait.
- The person who frequently is tight as a drum is seldom fit as a fiddle.

- The way to get in who's who is to know what's what.
- If you try to get something for nothing, you must be certain you don't end up getting nothing for something.
- People who live in glass houses have to answer the doorbell.
- The longer you carry a grudge, the heavier it gets.
- The happiest moment in life is when the folks back of you in the movies finish their popcorn.
- Some persons don't know the difference between thinking for you and thinking of yourself.
- Some people believe anything you tell them if you whisper it.
- As you grow older, you grow wiser, talk less and say more.
- The owner of a candid camera generally takes the worst view of everything.
- It's almost impossible to keep your mind and your mouth open at the same time.
- It's surprising how thoroughly you can be misinformed with a little reading.
- You are not really ignorant until somebody finds it out.
- A man is getting old when he starts letting his wife pick out his neckless.
- One advantage in being poor is that your closets aren't full of old clothes and junks.
- As a rule, a quitter isn't a very good beginner either.
- Flattery is falsehood to all but flattered.
- The straight and narrow path never crosses easy street.
- We have discovered that women used cosmetics in the middle ages. They still use them in the middle ages.
- We still think having money a little tight teaches sobriety to spenders.

- The Christmas coming is followed by the January billing.
- The family that isn't in debt today is underprivileged.
- Some students burn the midnight oil in the transmission instead of the lamp.
- The person who has too much money for his own good easily finds friends to share his misfortune.
- The world's choice Disarmament or disbursement.
- To be unhappily married requires a good income and to be incompatible a couple must be rich.
- Some persons never appeal to god unless they're getting licked.
- A telephone isn't a vacuum cleaner, but some people can get a lot of dirt out of it.
- No horse goes as fast as the money yet bet on him.
- All things come to him who crosses the street without looking.
- No matter how much money talks, most people don't find it boring.
- A good idea can get very lonely in an empty head.
- If you say you are less wise then you are, people will think you are wiser than you are.
- If you know you don't know much, you know more than most people.
- Some persons who are too proud to beg and too honest to steal, borrow and forget to pay.
- The person who tells you his troubles keep you from talking about yours.
- The only thing it's easy to do these days is to get confused.
- The grass on the other side of the fence may look greener, but is still has to be mowed once in a week.

- Modern man looks ahead to going to the moon, but hesitates to move to the rear of the bus.
- One reason a child must not suck his thumb is that he may need it someday.
- One trouble in this country is that too many persons try to get something for nothing, and trouble is that too many succeed.
- All men are born free and equal, and they stay that way up to the time they marry.
- Every once in a while you see one of nature's big mistakes "a small mind with a large mouth".
- The fellow who follows the horses generally finds the horses he follows follow other horses.
- Most of us who brag about what we are going to do tomorrow did the same thing yesterday.
- Money can't buy happiness, but there are some mighty attractive substitutes.
- Fun is expensive and the older you get, the more expensive it is.
- Nothing causes such interesting arguments as ignorance.
- Most of us can't stand prosperity, and the way we spend money we won't have to.
- Most of us make enough hay nowadays, but it's harder to stack it up.
- It's a smart child who can ask questions his parents can answer.
- There is nothing wrong with having nothing to say if you don't say it out loud.
- There are greater things in life than money, but the problem is convincing your wife.
- No one has more to learn that the person who knows everything.
- Nothing takes the starch out of you like a strict diet.

- Running into debt has its problems, but so does running into your creditors.
- If at first you don't succeed, you are like rest of us.
- Keep smiling and it may look as if you are not smart enough to understand the world's problems.
- The fellow who is a good sport has to lose to prove it.
- When you blow your top. You will make the best speech you will ever regret.
- If you get into deep water, the only safe course is to keep your mouth closed.
- A person seldom loses anything by good manners, but some people don't even take a chance.
- When you decide to know yourself, you may find the acquaintance isn't worth the effort.
- All of us are born in a state of ignorance and many of us never change residence.
- Money talks and in most families is the mother tongue.
- We have more high school and college graduates than ever before and fewer of them can read traffic signs.
- We live in a world of change, but it's hard to get your hands on any of it.
- The best speech you hear may be from the fellow who keeps his mouth shut.
- The average husband is worth about twice what his wife thinks of him and half what his mother thinks of him.
- Honesty pays, but not enough to satisfy some people.
- After dinner coffee is never so pleasant as when it is mixed with a little gossip.
- Few persons are so economical that they won't give you a piece of their mind.
- You can live a quite life just by living inside your income.
- Most of us dislike being reformed by someone who is not better than we are.

- It's very difficult to become famous by having common sense and good manners.
- When you ask whether something is worth what it costs, you'r getting old.
- One of the great mysteries to a married man is what a bachelor does with his time and money.
- Some people jump at conclusions while others dig for facts.
- Some people think life is dull if there isn't any place to go where they shouldn't be.
- Always put off until tomorrow the things you shouldn't do at all.
- Only a few people live on borrowed time compared to the number who live on borrowed money.
- A person who is alone isn't necessarily in good company.
- It makes a lot of difference in life whether you live and learn or just live.
- Many persons who din't save last month are certain they will next month.
- You are young only once but you can be immature all your life.
- When a thought strikes a person, no one can tell what will happen.
- The person who has nothing to say often proves it.
- No two persons are alike, and this makes it possible for each of us to be conceited.
- Travel doesn't broaden you as much as all the food you eat traveling.
- A feel and money can throw a lot of parties.
- "I think" is an overworked expression and almost always a gross exaggeration.

- It's not at his mother's knees but across them where a youngster learns his best lessons.
- Thee most difficult meal for a wife to get is breakfast in bed.
- If you want to get a job done, give it to a busy man and he will have his assistant do it.
- A person may know his own mind and still be ignorant.
- The man who has holes in his socks should wither get married or divorced.
- Nothing goes to a man's stomach like success.
- Sweet are the uses of your neighbour's adversity.
- Before a person tries his hand at something, he ought to try his head at it.
- A pessimist is a person who says all nations will share the atomic bomb.
- Sin is an old fashioned word used to describe what is now called sophistication.
- You can fool all the people some of the time, but you can fool yourself all the time.
- Half the word is always ready to tell the other half how to live.
- You seldom are so busy that you can't stop and tell others how busy you are.
- Most of us believe we are as good as we never were.
- Money makes fools of famous people, but it also makes famous people of fools.
- If you test a man's friendship by asking him to sign your note and he refuses, he is your friend.
- One advantage about blindness is that it requires very little attention.
- People who offer good advice always offer it in the big economy size.

- Some persons think there is no difference between self confidence and conceit.
- If all the officers in a business agree, some ot them aren't thinking.
- As you grow older, you stand for more and fall for less.
- A person has good manners if he is able to put us with bad ones in others.
- When a person is always right, there is something wrong.
- Every one has fun at the fat man's expense.
- The standard of living you can afford is the one you were on before you got your last raise.
- Every husband knows his words can flair you.
- an economist is a person who explains later how the thing he didn't expect was inevitable.
- If the months were made shorter, we wouldn't have so much months left over at the end of the money.
- Late to bed and early to rise makes you stupid rather than wise.
- One way to reduce blood pressure is to live within your income.
- Nothing is a better tranquilizer than a clear conscience.
- The fellow who follow the advice "Know thyself" is pretty certain not to tell anyone about it.
- Most of us enjoy defending a prejudice more than we do fighting for a principle.
- Punctuality is disappointing if no one is there to appreciate it.
- The next great advance in society will come when people become as speechless as they are thoughtless.
- The ant may be industrious, but he doesn't get on the front page as often as the butterfly.
- Truth in advertising: "The latest in antiques".

Little Red Book of Effective Speaking Skills   123

- A bird in hand is good, but it has wings.
- You can generally evade a difficult question with a long winded answer.
- "A penny saved is a penny earned" was true up to the invention of the sales tax.
- If you want to win friends and influence people, you have to lose arguments.
- The person who takes his time often takes yours too.
- A scientist says life is the metabolic activity of protoplasm, but is seems worse than that on Monday morning.
- Persons who say the boss is dumb would be out of a job if the boss were any smarter.
- It's great thing for a man to be married because he never has to worry about making his mind.
- One way to make others happy is to leave them alone.
- He who hesitates is last.
- A fool and his money get to go places.
- Sometimes you find a person who knows how to live everyone's life expertly but his own.
- It is always easy to see the silver lining in the other person's cloud.
- If you think you know it all, you haven't been listening.
- A man who is on a wild-goose chase all his life never feathers much of a nest.
- It's strange how conscience may hurt when everything else seems pretty good.
- Nothing is as easy as it looks except spending money and getting into an argument.
- Experience is what helps you to recognize everyone's mistakes expect your own.
- Schooldays are the happiest days parents have.

- Too many people determine what is right or wrong on the basis of which pays best.
- It's bad enough to make fool of yourself, but it's worse if you don't know who did it.
- A hobby is something you go nuts about to keep from going nuts about what you are doing.
- A husband may read his wife like a book, but he can't shut her up that easily.
- Don't complain about getting old, because when you stop you are dead.
- Marriage is a mutual partnership if both parties know when to be mute.
- A generation ago most men who finished a hard day's work needed rest.
- There are five thousand languages and dialects in the world, and money speaks all of them.
- Doctors say you should lie on the right side. We agree, if you must lie, always lie on the right side.
- Most of us say no to temptation once weakly.
- One trouble with the world is that there are too many clowns that aren't in the circus.
- Money doesn't make you happy, but it certainly quiets your nerves.
- A person who is overweight is living beyond his seams.
- An old master is an artist who could paint almost as well as those who have since copied his paintings.
- What the world needs is not people to rewrite the Bible, but people to re-read it.
- Too many people think work is a good thing if it doesn't take up too much of your spare time.
- The person who always insists on speaking his mind doesn't necessarily have one.

- Friendship is what makes you think almost as much of someone else as you do of yourself.
- There are a great many books now on how to live longer, but none on why.
- Public opinion is simply the private opinion of one person who made enough noise to attract some converts.
- With some married couples the big difference of opinion is whether he earns too little or she spends too much.
- Obstacles are the terrible things you see when you take your eyes from the goal.
- Two can live as cheaply as one, and after marriage they do.
- Anger gets us into trouble because it makes the mouth move faster than the brain.
- A smart husband doesn't go home and complain about dinner, but takes his wife to a restaurant where they can both complain.
- Foresight is knowing when to close your mouth before someone suggests it.
- The only person more stupid than the person who thinks he knows it all is the person who argues with him.
- No man with money is short of cousins.
- A slip of the tongue will often cause greater damage than a slip of the foot.
- If you rest your chin on your hand when you think, it will help you to keep your mouth closed.
- Unless you can look interested when you are bored, you will never be a success socially.
- A man who is always on the go often never gets there.
- Some people consider nothing is a luxury if they can afford it.
- Most of us spend a great deal of time just letting off esteem..

Round Up

1. In one concise sentence, what is the purpose of this speech?
2. Who is the audience? What is their main interest in this topic?
3. What do I really know and believe about this topic as it relates to this audience?
4. What additional research can I do?
5. What are the main points of this presentation?
6. What supporting information and stories can I use to support each of my main points?
7. What visual aids, if any, do I need?
8. Do I have an effective opening grabber?
9. In my final summary, how will I plan to tell them "What's In It For Me?"
10. Have I polished and prepared the language and words I will use?
11. Have I prepared a written and concise introduction for myself?
12. Have I taken care of the little details that will help me speak more confidently?

Part III

Shut Up

Know when to shut up. Leave your audience wanting for more. Don't say 'Finally' and keep speaking.

How to Polish Your Speaking Skills: It's Time for T.I.P.S.

Many people will do just about anything to avoid public speaking. Or, you may have said "Who's got the time?" or "That's not good use of my time." Therein lies the issue- it's all about time!

**The best public speakers make the time to learn about their audience so that what they're saying is what the audience is interested in hearing.

****The best public speakers know that timing is everything.** They find out exactly what their speaking time allotment is, and then practice getting their timing right so they don't run over or run short.

The best public speakers appreciate the **value of time out. They leave a **"cushion" of time** before and after they speak, to reduce stage fright.

**The best public speakers recognize the third time's a charm. On average you'll want to practice your presentation aloud three times to work on your opening and closing, your nonverbal language and your intonation.

The best public speakers are aware that **time marches on. While the initial 30-60 seconds of a presentation seem like hours due to an elevated stress level, it quickly subsides as you proceed with your purpose and remember that the audience is there because they need what you have.

Finally, there's no time like the present to work on your T.I.P.S., which by the way represents **Talking Is Public Speaking**. Every time you speak, it's a form of public speaking. Isn't it about time?

Stand up, speak up, shut up

Good luck.